Micr

MW01533950

Pro 7 User Guide

The Complete User Guide to Help You Master the

New Microsoft Surface Pro 7

Sam O. Wealth

Contents

Introduction

You're welcome to this guide. With this guide, you can transform Surface Pro 7 into a working horse, thanks to the included Kickstand and Surface Signature Type Cover.

You can even leverage the included the USB-C and USB-A ports to connect to docking stations, displays and your accessories. The best part is that you will enjoy all-day battery, fast charging, and instant On with this flagship device.

The Music sounds is crisp and clear, thanks to the Dolby Audio Premium sound. You can even take advantage of your next call or use voice dictation with the dual-far-field Studio Mics.

Another perk is that you can do much more with the Windows you know. Yes, you will get to use familiar features like Windows Microsoft Edge, Hello sign-in and use the Office 365 to create your finest work and store it in OneDrive safely.

How to Setup Microsoft Surface Pro 7

You will need an email address to get started. Once you have this, you will be able to access the following:

- Free online storage.
- An online password reset for your surface pro 7.
- And many more with the Microsoft account.

Create a Microsoft Account

By registering your surface to a Microsoft account, you will be able to keep track of the details as regards the warranty of your device including getting technical support irrespective of wherever you are.

● You will also get free access to your Office Online, Skype, Outlook, OneDrive, OneNote and many more.

● You will also have access to more fun with the Microsoft Store and Xbox Live as well as personalizing them to your interest.

● Signing in with Microsoft also gets you easily in touch with your favorite games, apps, movies, music, etc.

● When signed in with Microsoft, you will also get to redeem points for movies, gift cards, games, and music or charity donations.

● You are required to take the following steps to register your Microsoft surface device.

i Go to the link: https://devicesupport.microsoft.com
If where you are already signed in, your profile name and icon will appear at the top corner of the page. After you sign in, you can move ahead to the next step. But if you are not signed in, you will need to select the sign in from the top corner by inputting your Microsoft account credentials.

If you don't have a Microsoft account yet, select the Sign-up option to create a Microsoft account. To have your device registered, it's mandatory for you to have a Microsoft account.

ii. As soon as you are signed in to your Microsoft account, you will be redirected back to the Device support where you will have Help with device registration, warranty info as well as the service page.

iii. Select "**Register my device**" which will be found under the Overview section at the right of the "My Devices" option and then the registration process can begin.

iv. In a situation where you don't have any registered devices, go to My Devices, just below this, you will find a blue **Get Started button** which you will need to click on to start the registration process.

v. You will be prompted with the Register your Microsoft Device page.

vi. Select your Country/Region from the drop-down menu that comes up.

vii. From the drop-down menu, select your product family type.

viii. Input in your Serial number in the Serial number box that is available on the Registration page.

ix. Click the checkbox to accept the terms of the privacy statement.

x. Select the blue Register button. Once the surface has been successfully registered, you will be prompted with a message which says" Success! You registered your device successfully"

xi. To view and manage your registered device, select the Device Support at the top of the page.

Set up Windows Hello

You can also get instant access to your Surface Pro device with Windows Hello. To do that:

You have to: Go to Start ■ > Settings ⚙ > Accounts ⌂ > Sign-in options.

Below Windows Hello, choose Set up.

Getting Started with Office

Activate Office 365, 2019, 2016, and 2013

When you install Office in your device, the "Sign in to set up Office" page may appear.

Once you start an Office app that is not yet activated, you will be guided to sign in to Office. Make sure you sign in by using:

1. The Microsoft account
2. School or work account
3. The particular account that you used to buy
4. Or subscribed to Office.

Take note that if Office came already installed on your new device, check for "**Activate Office**" that is pre-installed on a new Windows 10 device.

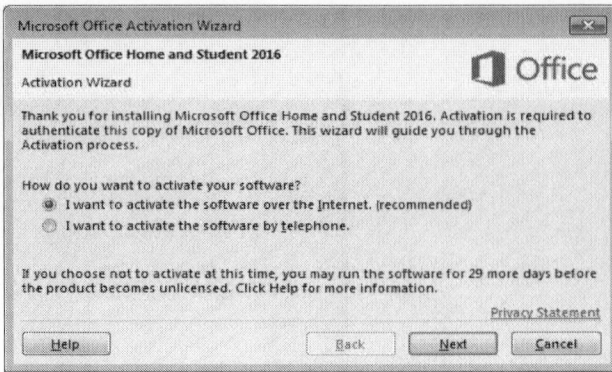

What shows next in your device is the "**Microsoft Office Activation Wizard**"

If the Activation Wizard appears, you will need to activate Office.Then follow the instructions in the wizard to help you activate Office. With the help of the Activation wizard, you will be able to activate Office successfully on your device.

You are to activate the Office that is pre-installed on the new Windows 10 device

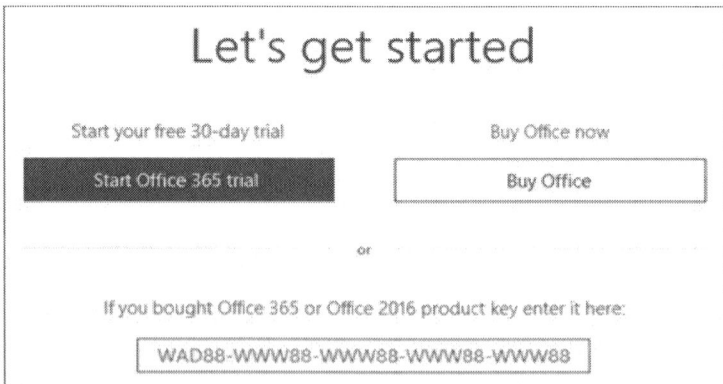

If you see the above screen appear on your new device, know that Office is installed as an Office 365 Home trial.

And you will only see this screen if you sign in to the Office that was pre-installed on your new device. Meaning, you still don't have an Office product associated with your account.

For you to use Office on your new device, you need to activate Office as a 1-month trial of Office 365 Home.

Note the following: You can buy Office, you can also add Office to an existing Office 365 subscription, or enter a product key from a new product key card. And if you have an older version of Office, you can install that as well.

Office purchase should be activated or the offer that's included on a new Windows 10 device

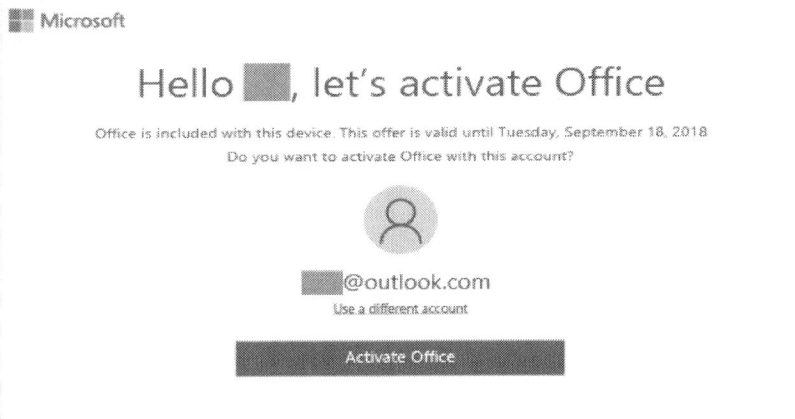

You may find this prompt on your screen "The products we found in your account can't be used to activate <app>" If you see this on your screen, know that Office is installed as a one (1)-year subscription or one-time purchase.

Also a digital Office product key is sent to your PC, what that means is that you won't need or receive a printed product key. How you activate Office is by clicking on the Activate Office button. Ensure you activate Office early enough, as the offer will last for only 180 days after you activate Windows and thereafter it will expire.

Ensure to get the necessary help while activating an Office purchase or free offer on a new PC

Do activate the Office HUP

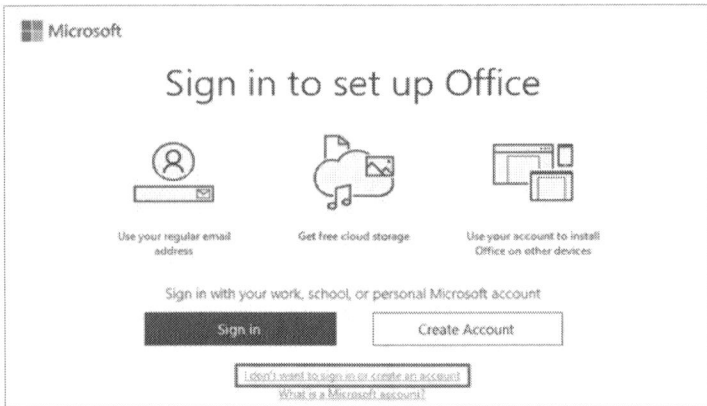

Microsoft

Sign in to set up Office

Use your regular email address | Get free cloud storage | Use your account to install Office on other devices

Sign in with your work, school, or personal Microsoft account

Sign in | Create Account

I don't want to sign in or create an account
What is a Microsoft account?

If you acquired a Visio Professional or an Office Professional Plus, or a Project Professional through your Microsoft HUP employer's benefit, click on "**I don't want to sign i**n" option or open an account option below the screen of your device and then put in your product key. Make sure you get your HUP product key

How to Activate A Brand New Office Product Key

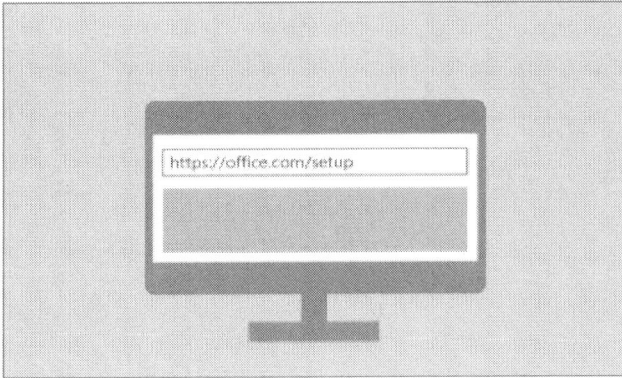

In case you purchased a new Office product key card, or you received a product key when you purchased Office through an e-store, go to Office.com/setup and follow the instructions that pops up on the screen. This process is carried out once, and your new Office product will be added to your Microsoft account. Once you gain possession of your key, you can easily install Office.

With Office.com/setup you can get all the help you need to install Office.

Office should be activated if you see a "limit reached" error

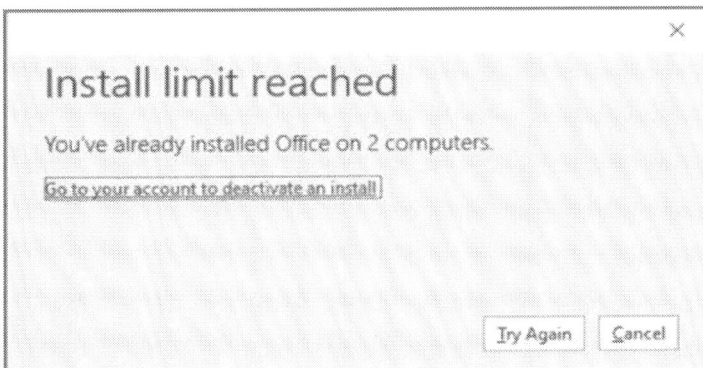

If this message pops up on your screen, what it means is that you have to deactivate or better still sign out of Office using another device before you can activate Office again on your own device. First deactivate Office 365 to re-activate it on your new device.

Troubleshoot Activation Errors

If Office could not be activated, it will eventually become an unlicensed tool and thereafter all the editing features of Office will be disabled. There are different factors that can make Office to become unlicensed.

For instance, in the event that your Office 365 subscription expires, you have to renew your subscription so that all features of Office can be restored.

In case Office has already been pre-installed on your new device (PC), you have to start an Office 365 Home trial or buy Office for you to continue using Office.

A subscription notice will appear when you open an Office 365 application

In case you get an Office error that says "The products we found in your account can't be used to activate <app>"

You have to troubleshoot activation errors in Office to be able to activate it.

How to Update Surface Firmware and Windows 10

There are two types of updates that will keep your Surface to function perfectly:

(a) Surface updates for hardware, also known as firmware,

(b) Windows 10 software updates.

These two types of update usually get installed automatically once they become available. If you have any questions or difficulty with an update, here's some info that might help.

We would go through the update process for a Surface device that's running Windows 10 starting with preparation of your device and internet connection.

Before You Start Updating

Add your Surface Type Cover or Surface docking station (if you are in possession of one) so that it can get the most recent updates, too.

Ensure you have a stable internet connection, Wi-Fi or Ethernet will be preferable, because they are the best for downloading. If you are having difficulty in installing updates, it may be because of a connection problem. You can fix the network connection issues in Windows. If you are unable to use Wi-Fi, below are a few alternatives for you:

- Use an Ethernet connection with the Surface Dock or Ethernet to USB adapter.

- If you are in possession of an LTE-enabled device, turn off Set as metered connection to get all updates over your mobile broadband connection. Get help with metered internet connections.

Your Surface should be plugged into an outlet. Also ensure your Surface is charged to at least 40 percent before you start installing updates. Make sure your Surface is kept plugged in and turn it on while it is updating.

Update Windows 10

After you have followed the preparation steps, click the Windows updates to see all the available updates and choose your options.

Update Surface Drivers and Firmware

Next thing to do after following the preparation steps, and if you are not able to check the Windows Update, you should download "update files" manually for any Surface device.

For you to select and update your Surface device, check the Download drivers and firmware for Surface.

Take note that the time for installation varies, and it depends largely on the speed of your internet connection, the number of updates to be done, and also the size of the update files.

Problems Installing Updates?

If you are having any other issues trying to install Surface driver/firmware updates, look for Trouble installing Surface updates?

More Update Info

To know more about the Surface updates released so far, check for Surface update history.

For you to know which Windows and Surface updates you've already installed, click on Windows Update: FAQ, How do I see installed updates on my PC?

In case you are searching for Windows 10 updates on a PC, instead of Surface, you can check Update Windows 10.

Surface storage

Take note that some products might not be available in your country or region.

Also note that pre-installed software, apps, and updates use a large amount of the internal disk space on your Surface.

How Much Disk Space Do I Have?

The type of Surface you have is what determines the amount of free disk space that will be available for your music, photos, videos, and other contents. The space available might also differ depending on the country or region you live in and also depending on the languages and apps that are pre-installed in the device.

How Can I Add Storage Space?

You can use any of the under-listed storage options, in case you need more storage space for your device:

- **OneDrive**: You can save your files on 'OneDrive', that is the free cloud storage which comes along with your Microsoft account.
- **SD card**: Some Surface may have slot for SD or microSD card, if your Surface has the slot, insert your memory card into the card slot on your Surface.

- **USB flash drive or hard drive**: Another option is to insert a USB flash drive or a hard drive into the USB port that is provided on your Surface.

What Software And Apps Come With My Surface?

There are apps that will help you get information, give you entertainment, help you stay connected, and become productive. These apps come along with your Surface, pre-installed and ready to use.

How to Navigate with the use of your Surface Touchscreen

Swipe from the right to have quick changes made

From the action center, you can get to quickly see notifications or alter things such as the network, Airplane mode and Bluetooth. To do this, just take a swipe from the right side of the surface of your touch screen.

Switch between apps by swiping from left to right

- Swipe in from the left side of the touchscreen of your surface and select your desired app to get access to view all your apps and switch quickly between the apps as well.
- You can also get to close an app from the Task menu.

Swiping down from the top to resize or see the title bar

- In a situation where an app is maximized, you can make it smaller by swiping down from the top of the Surface touchscreen.

- When an app is in a full-screen mode, such as the OneNote, to view the title bar; swipe down to display the title.

Swipe up from the bottom to view the Taskbar

- You can swipe up from the bottom of the touch screen of your surface to access the taskbar in a situation where an app is in full screen.

- You can tap anywhere on the touch screen to hide the app as well.

Select and open things with a tap

With the use of your finger, and tapping on an item on the touch screen of your Surface, you will get to select things or have apps opened just like your mobile device.

Tap and hold to get more info

- Press down with the use of your finger.

- Hold down for a second to get details about the item or open up the menu, this is similar to making use of the right click with your mouse.

Zoom in and out by pinching or stretching

- To zoom in and out on your device, place two of your fingers on the touch screen of your surface.

- To zoom in, you will move the two fingers away from each other.

16

- To zoom out, you will move the two fingers towards each other.

Dragging up and down to scroll

- With the use of your finger, you can get to scroll vertically or horizontally just like on your smartphone.
- All you need to do is drag your finger up and down on your touch screen.

Pressing and dragging to move

- Your finger can be used to select items.
- Press and hold the item with your finger to drag the item to a new spot.

Swipe to Select

- You can select things quickly by making use of your finger on the surface touch screen.
- Swipe with a quick flick to have an item selected.

Clean and care for your Surface

In order to keep your Surface looking and working fine, endeavor to clean the touchscreen and keyboard as often as possible, also keep your Surface covered when it's not in use.

Listed below are ways to maintain and keep your Surface in good condition:

- General cleaning
- Cover and Keyboard care
- Power cord care
- Battery health
- Alcantara® material care
- Touchscreen care.

General Cleaning Recommendations

For your Surface to continue to look great and work perfectly, make sure you use a soft lint-free cloth (microfiber cloths would be best) soak it in a little quantity of mild soap and water, or screen wipes. Ensure to clean it every 3-6 months or whenever it becomes necessary.

Warning: Never apply liquids directly to your Surface.

Cover And Keyboard Care

Only a little amount of effort is needed for you to keep the Touch Cover or the Type Cover working at its best. For proper cleaning, soak a lint-free cloth in mild soap and water and wipe the cover with it.

Take Note: Do not apply liquids directly to your Surface or to the cover. Ensure you do proper cleaning always to keep your Touch Cover or Type Cover looking good.

Peradventure the spine or magnetic connections of your cover become dirty or get stained, use a little quantity of isopropyl alcohol (which is also called rubbing alcohol) then use a soft, lint-free cloth to clean it.

Battery Health

Rechargeable batteries do not last forever, they all eventually wear out with time. Below are a few tips on how to make your batteries last longer.

• In a month, allow your battery to drain at least below half way before charging it.

• Do not leave your Surface plugged in 24/7.

• Keep your Surface stored in a cool and dry room when it's not in use.

If you intend to keep your Surface stored for a longer period of time, get it charged up to 50% every six months to ensure it stays chargeable.

Touchscreen Care

Your touchscreen performance can be affected by scratches, finger grease, dust, chemicals, and ultraviolet light. Thus, listed below are a few things you can do to help protect the screen:

1. Clean Often. The Surface touchscreen is coated to make it simple to clean. You do not require so much effort to get rid of fingerprints or oily spots. Use a soft, lint-free fabric (either dry or soaked with water) or (monocle cleaner—Do not use glass or any other chemical cleaners) alternatively use a screen cleaning wipe to carefully wipe stains off the screen.

2. Keep away from sun. Never leave your Surface under direct sunlight d

3. For a long period of time, because ultraviolet light and excessive heat can easily affect the display.

4. Keep it covered. The cover must be kept closed whenever you are taking your Surface along with you, or if you're not using it.

Alcantara® Material Care

Some versions of Surface devices and their accessories do feature spill and absorption-resistant Alcantara® material.

Regular Care

For the Alcantara to be in perfect condition, do clean it with a lint-free white fabric soaked in a mixture of mild soap and water or use a screen cleaning wipe as the case may be.

Stain Removal

If the Alcantara material gets stained, make efforts to clean it within the shortest possible time, at least within 30 minutes to help prevent any stains from permanently setting on it. Try to use swirling motions to softly clean with a white lint-free cloth that has been soaked with mild soap and water. You can make solution of two parts, one part of water and the other part of mild soap (hand soap will do). Wipe dry using a clean light-colored cloth.

Power Cord Care

Like any other metal wire or cable, Power cords, can be weakened or destroyed if it gets twisted or bent continuously in the same spot. Some few tips have been given below on what should do to keep your power cord from getting destroyed:

• **Avoid twisting or pinching your power cord.**

• Do not wrap your power cord too firmly, particularly around the power brick. Rather, wrap it by using loose coils instead of tight angles.

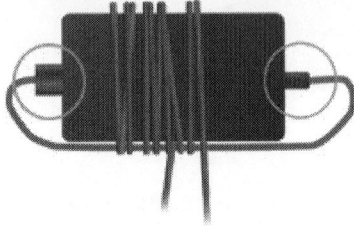

Correct: Cord wrapped loosely

Incorrect: Cord wrapped too tightly

• Check your power cord always, particularly where it joins with the power brick.

• Do not pull the power cord when unplugging your Surface. By carefully removing the connector from the charging connector you can prevent your power cord from getting damaged.

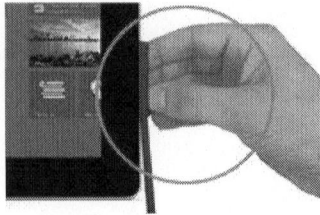

Correct: Unplugging gently

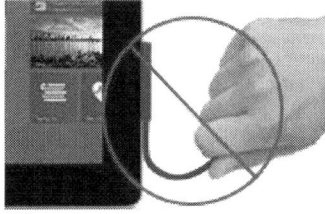

Incorrect: Tugging on cord to unplug

If you discover any part of your Surface chargers cords damaged, stop using the cord and contact the manufacturer for necessary support.

What to Do If Your Surface Touchscreen Doesn't Work

If you are having issues with your Surface touchscreen, (physical damage to the screen inclusive), need touchscreen drivers or firmware, or want to remove touch on your Surface, explore the following solutions.

Identify Your Issue

Choose your issue to get more elaborate description. If any matches your issue, click on the recommended solution link.

Take note: If instead of Surface, you're using another Windows 10 device, these steps will not work for you. In that case, reach out to your Windows 10 device manufacturer for troubleshooting support.

If touch does not respond on all or part of the screen

- When you press certain spots, or anywhere on the screen, nothing happens.

- If neither multitouch (pinch-to-zoom, for example) nor single-touch gestures work.
- If the Pen inking does not work.
- And if clicking other mouse actions, and typing all work.

The best solution to the above is Standard Touchscreen Troubleshooting

Multi-touch gestures don't work or touch is inaccurate

- If the Multi-touch gestures such as pinch-to-zoom and swiping don't work.
- If the Single-touch gestures like scrolling and tapping to open apps work.
- If Pen inking does not work.
- If clicking other mouse actions, and typing all work.
- And if when you touch the screen, another part of the screen responds, e.g if you tap the right side of the screen and something on the left side of the screen responds.

Standard touchscreen troubleshooting is the recommended solution.

Touch is slow to respond

- If when you tap to open an app or file, the app or file delays before it opens.

- If the Touch input takes a while before it responds.

The recommended solution is to improve Surface performance

It is important to note that Touch performance depends on your device's ability to process actions and tasks, not on its touchscreen.

Your Surface experiences "phantom" touches, this occurs if:

- Your Surface acts as if someone is touching the screen, but in actual fact no one is.
- If white dots appear on part or all of the screen.
- If phantom touches interfere with mouse actions, clicking, or typing.

How to disable touch on Surface

• If you want to disable all touch functionality on your Surface,

• Note that if you disable touch other touch accessories such as Surface Pen, Surface Dial, and Windows Touch Keyboard will be disabled too.

The recommended solution is to enable and disable your touchscreen in Windows 10

If the Surface Pen doesn't ink

• If when you try to use Surface Pen to draw or ink on Surface the pen does not ink, and it's not recognized by the Surface.

• Also, your Surface touchscreen may not work.

The solution recommended is to troubleshoot Microsoft Surface Pen

If the Surface Touch driver or firmware is missing from Device Manager

• Another problem may be when you open Device Manager, and you don't see Surface Touch firmware listed.

• Or the HID-Compliant Touchscreen driver is not found in the Device Manager.

• Or if you have a yellow bang or error close to Surface Touch firmware or drivers that are listed in Device Manager.

Standard touchscreen troubleshooting is the recommended solution or better still Download drivers and firmware for Surface.

Cracked Screen or Other Physical Damage

If your Surface touchscreen gets damaged. This includes cracking, bubbling, blemishes, and any other physical issues. The solution is to check for Surface cracked screen or physical damage.

Warning

While troubleshooting your device, it may be recommended that your Surface must be reset or changed. To know more about how to back up your data, check "Back up the data on your Surface".

Standard Touchscreen Troubleshooting

If your keyboard or mouse is not connected? Based on your issue, you might not be able to perform these steps. It is recommended for you to use a Surface Type Cover, USB keyboard or mouse, or Bluetooth keyboard or mouse.

Solution 1: Check for Windows and Surface updates

1. Go to **Start** > **Settings** > **Update & Security** > **Windows Update** > **Check for updates.**

2. Once you have installed the updates, at the right under **Windows Update,** click on **Restart now**. Your Surface may restart several times, this depends on the updates that were installed.

For you to know whether this solution solved the issue, use touch to open an application that is like Microsoft Edge or use another web browser, then try to scroll, pinch to zoom, swipe in from the right, and long-press to test the touch functionality. If your touchscreen fails to work after you do this, go on to Solution 2.

Tip

Are you having difficulties in getting updates? Or do you want to run your Surface through diagnostics? For you to fix Windows Update issues and to access a suite of tests for your Surface, look out for the Surface Diagnostic Toolkit.

No. 2 Solution is to Boot to UEFI and test touch functionality

Unified Extensible Firmware Interface (UEFI) is a type of software that enables Windows to communicate with your Surface's hardware. And because UEFI operates independently of Windows, to test hardware in UEFI will work if you have any hardware issue. For instance, if touch does not work in UEFI, your device most likely has developed a hardware failure and would need servicing.

In case the touch works in UEFI, the problem may likely involve Windows or the touch driver. Then follow the steps below to boot to UEFI and test if the touch is functioning well:

1. Go to **Start** > **Power** > **Shut down.**

2. When Surface goes off, tap and hold the button for volume up and then click on the power button until a Microsoft or Surface logo shows up on the screen.

3. When you are in UEFI, tap your Surface screen and check if it responds normally. Try to learn more in UEFI by clicking on various menu items. Also, depending on how your Surface responds to touch, follow one of these steps:

• If touch does not work on your Surface, your touchscreen may possibly have experienced a hardware problem. Open Device service and repair to submit a service order for your Surface. If you want to work with a Surface Support Advocate, reach out to us.

• If touch works on your Surface, click on **EXIT**, follow any instructions that pops on the screen, and restart Windows. Then move to Solution 3.

Solution 3: Reinstall the touchscreen driver

1. Open the search box on the taskbar and type in **device manager**, then choose **Device Manager** in the results that pops up.

2. Enlarge the **Human Interface Devices** category.

3. Right-click on **HID-compliant touch screen**, select **Uninstall device**, and then, in the **Uninstall Device** dialog box, click **Uninstall**. In case you see two HID-compliant touch screen drivers, right-click the first one, tap on **Uninstall device**, choose **Uninstall**, and then do the process again for the second driver.

Note: If no HID-compliant touch screen driver on the listed, go to Solution 5.

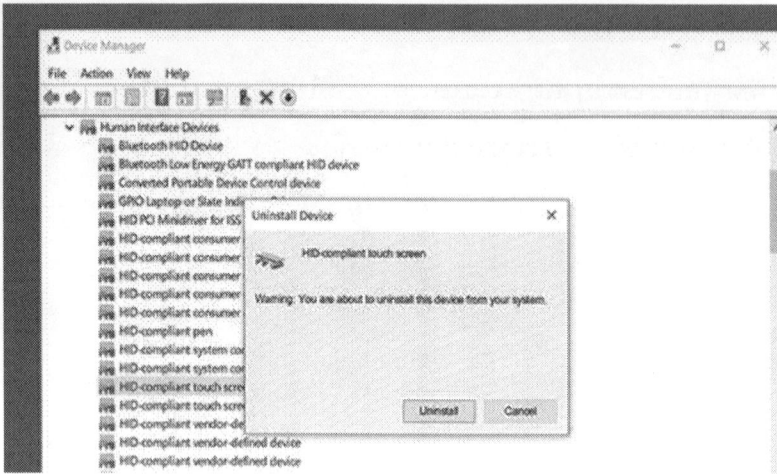

4. Re-start your Surface and it will automatically download and install the touchscreen driver when you connect to the internet.

5. You should use touch to open an application that is like Edge or use another web browser, and then try to scroll, pinch to zoom, swipe in from the right, and long-press to test touch functionality. If you are still having issues, move on to Solution 4.

Solution 4: The touch calibration should be reset to the default settings

Warning!

Don't recalibrate your touch settings manually. The Surface devices are already calibrated and optimized as they come from the factory, for pen and touch input to ensure they function perfectly. If your Surface gets recalibrated by someone manually or its default calibration changed, you may have issues with your device.

1. In the search box on the taskbar, type in **calibrate**, and then click on **Calibrate the screen for pen or touch input** from the results displayed. (Use your mouse to click on **Start**, go on to select **Calibrate the screen for pen or touch input**.)

2. Click Tab until you have selected **Reset**, then tap **Enter**. (In case you are using a mouse, choose **Reset.**) If **Reset** is not available know that your Surface touch calibration is at the factory settings. So move to the 5th Solution.

3. Click **Tab** until you have selected **Yes**, tap **Enter**, and comply with the instructions displayed on the screen to recalibrate your Surface. (If using a mouse, click on **Yes**, and also follow the instructions on the screen to recalibrate your Surface.)

4. To check whether your touchscreen responds appropriately, restart your Surface and test the touchscreen.

Also to know whether this solution solved the problem, use touch to open an application like Edge or another web browser, and then make an attempt to scroll, pinch to zoom, swipe in from the right, and long-press to test the touch functionality.

If you still have issues, move on to Solution 5.

For Solution 5, you can either restore or reset Surface or create and use a USB recovery drive.

When you reach this point, you must recognize that the Surface device is not the issue. Use the table below to know which reset option is appropriate for your situation.

Recovery type	What it does	How it impacts you
Restore or reset Surface	This method puts the device back to its factory settings, exactly as it was when you first took it out of the box. It uses a version of Windows that's stored on your hard drive. This works well if there are no issues with the version of Windows stored on your hard drive.	• Data loss will occur • Settings will go back to factory defaults • You must reinstall both desktop and Windows Store apps • You will probably need to install updates after the reset

Create and use a USB recovery drive	This is the most thorough recovery method. It completely reinstalls the version of Windows that's stored on the hard drive of your Surface device.	• Data loss will occur • Settings will go back to factory defaults • You must reinstall both desktop and Windows Store apps • You will probably need to install updates after the reset • You will need to have a USB drive

Once you complete the reset and device setup, go on and use touch to open an application like Edge or another web browser, make attempt to scroll pinch to zoom, swipe in from the right, and long-press to test if the touch is functioning well.

If the reset option solved the issue, know that something changed in your device's software that caused the touchscreen not work properly. If you add more programs and apps to your device, do check if your touchscreen is functioning well.

Ensure to install all available updates for your Surface after you do a reset.

If you are still having the same issue, your touchscreen most likely have experienced a hardware failure. So go to Device service and repair it to start a service order for your Surface.

Troubleshoot Surface Screen Rotation

Take Note: there are some products that might not be available in your country or area.

Surface is created to change the display automatically as you turn it so that what you see on the screen will always be right side up. If the display doesn't rotate automatically, try the under-listed solutions in their order.

• Solution 1: First disconnect your Surface Cover and any external displays

• Solution 2: Then check the auto-rotation setting

• Solution 3: Also turn your Surface off and back on

• Solution 4: Then install the latest updates

• Solution 5: Next is to run a troubleshooter

• Solution 6: And finally restore Surface

Solution 1 is to disconnect your Surface Cover and any external displays

The Surface is setting created to display the screen in landscape orientation any time you're typing on a Surface Type Cover or your Surface is connected to an external display.

1. So disconnect your Surface Typing Cover and any external displays to know if they are stopping your screen from auto-rotating.

2. Also check to find out if your Surface display auto-rotates when you turn your Surface.

If the screen still does not auto-rotate, explore **Solution 2.**

Solution 2: Check the auto-rotation setting

If you see that the screen does not auto-rotate, it's possible the auto-rotation setting may be locked in one position. See how to unlock it below:

1. After the Cover has been detached, swipe in from the right edge of the screen, or select **Action center Notification icon** in the taskbar.

2. If **Rotation lock** is not dimmed, it means auto-rotation is locked. So select **Rotation lock** to unlock auto-rotation.

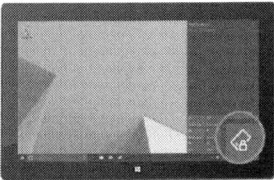

Take Note

The Rotation lock is undimmed when auto-rotation is locked. And when auto-rotation is locked, the screen will not rotate when you change the orientation of your Surface.

3. Attach your Surface Typing Cover again, then fold it back, and check whether the display rotates by itself when you turn your Surface.

Note the following:

• The screen rotation on Surface locks automatically when an attached Surface Typing Cover is in a typing position.

• Folding back your Surface Typing Cover will enable the screen to auto-rotate, unless auto-rotation on your Surface is locked.

• And if your Surface screen is in portrait position, as at the time you attach your Surface Typing Cover or when you connect an external display, the screen will rotate by itself to landscape orientation, even when the auto-rotation is locked.

Now, if the auto-rotation still doesn't work after you have unlocked auto-rotation, try **Solution 3.**

Solution 3 requires you to turn your Surface off and back on

1. Move to **Start** , and tap **Power > Shut down.**

2. Then click the power button on your Surface to turn it back on.

3. Lastly sign in to Windows and check to see if the display rotates automatically when you turn your Surface.

If after turning your Surface off and turning it back on does not help, try the next solution (**Solution 4**).

Solution 4: Install the latest updates

Try to Install the latest updates for your Microsoft Surface, and include updates to Windows and the accelerometer or other sensors, these may help fix the rotation problem.

And if the auto-rotation still doesn't work after installing updates, go to the next solution (**Solution 5**).

Solution 5: Run a troubleshooter

Go to the Sensors Troubleshooter. In the **File Download** dialog box, press **Open**, and follow the instructions that appear.

If this solution does not work, move to **Solution 6.**

Solution 6: Restore Surface

If the problems with auto-rotation still persist, try to restore your Surface. Know that restoring your Surface is a way to cancel recent system changes that may be causing you problems. And restoring Surface doesn't change your personal files, but it may remove newly installed apps and drivers.

Troubleshoot Connecting Surface to A Second Screen

Note again that some products might not be available in your country or location.

Before you start troubleshooting

Note that in most instances, downloading and installing the latest updates for Windows and your Surface will fix many problems. Another possible solution is to unplug your monitor from the power outlet and then plug it back in.

Setting Up Your Multiple-Monitor Desktop

Identify your device in this table to enable you find what you need to set up a second monitor with your Surface device.

My Surface device	Daisy chain support	External display/audio output port
Surface Pro		
Surface Studio	Yes	Mini DisplayPort
Surface Laptop		
Surface Book		
Surface Book 2		
Surface Studio 2	Yes	USB-C
Surface Go		
Surface 3	No	Mini DisplayPort

Take Note that for the USB-C to HDMI adapter, it is recommended to use the HDMI adapter with a HDMI 2.0 cable or higher. Also note that HDMI connections can transmit audio signals. So it is recommended that you use Microsoft's USB-C adapters on the devices equipped with the USB-C port.

Troubleshooting Solutions

If you are having issues connecting your Surface to a TV, monitor, or projector, try the listed solutions to fix the issue.

• Solution 1: Check the video input settings on the external screen

• Solution 2: Duplicate or extend your display onto your external screen

• Solution 3: Check the video cables

• Solution 4: Check the display adapter

• Solution 5: Clear your display cache

• Solution 6: Change the supported resolution and refresh rates

• Solution 7: Check your monitor's compatibility

• Solution 8: The adapter should be tested on a different external display

• Solution 9: Try out any of these possibilities if you have a wireless display.

No. 1 Solution is to Check the video input settings on the external screen

If your Surface is connected to a second screen and you don't see any video output from your Surface, the issue may be with the source selection or video input settings on the second screen, i.e if you're using an HDMI connection to a second screen, the second screen must recognize HDMI as the video input signal.

If you want to change the video input setting on your second screen, follow strictly the information provided in the manual for the screen or visit the manufacturer's website.

The common video input settings are VGA, DVI, AUX, DisplayPort, HDMI, Line in, Input, and Source.

After checking the input settings on the second screen, if it still doesn't work, try **Solution 2.**

Solution 2 is to Duplicate or extend your display to your external screen

Press **Windows key +P** on your keyboard, or select the **action center Notification icon** on the taskbar, and click on**Project**.

If you want to:	Choose:
See things only on your Surface display.	PC screen only
See the same things on both your Surface display and on the TV, monitor, or projector. To learn more about screen resolutions, go to Solution 6.	Duplicate
Move what's on the screen across your Surface display and onto the TV or monitor screen. When you have displays extended, you can drag and move items between the two screens and select a different resolution for your second screen. To learn more about screen resolutions, go to Solution 6.	Extend
See everything on the second screen. The display on your Surface will be blank.	Second screen only
All models of Surface Studio, Surface Book, Surface Go, Surface Pro, Surface Laptop, and Surface 3 can wirelessly connect to compatible displays by using Miracast.	Connect to a wireless display

If you could not get the results in the second screen, go to **Solution 3.**

Solution 3: Check the video cables

Make sure you use a video cable that is not longer than 6 feet (1.8 meters) because if the cables are too long they can affect your video quality. Make sure all your video connections are protected. Check the connection from the USB-C port, Mini DisplayPort on your Surface, or docking station, also check any video adapter you are using, and the connection on the video port on your TV, monitor, or projector.

• The cable that came with your monitor is what you should use, alternatively, check if the cable supports video. And make sure you do this always with Surface devices with USB-C ports.

• If the cable that followed your monitor does not respond, use another type of video cable to connect your Surface.

• If what you are using is video extension cable or video converter, take it away from your set up to see if that's the cause of the problem.

• And if what you are using is a video adapter from a different company and you're having issues with it, reach out to the adapter's manufacturer for assistance.

In case your monitor is good for DisplayPort, it is recommended for you to use a Mini DisplayPort-to-DisplayPort cable which should not be more than 6 feet (1.8 meters) long. With DisplayPort you can use the highest supported resolution and refresh rate with your Surface. These mini Display Port to DisplayPort cables functions best with a DisplayPort monitor:

• StarTech® 6 ft Mini DisplayPort to DisplayPort 1.2 Adapter Cable (model MDP2DPMM6)

• StarTech® 6 ft DisplayPort to DisplayPort 1.2 Cable with Latches (for daisy-chain) (model DISPLPORT6L)

If you are making a daisy chain multiple monitors, this is what you need:

• You need two monitors with DisplayPort 1.2 input ports and a minimum of one DisplayPort output port.

• And standard DisplayPort cables with a minimum of one Mini DisplayPort end

If your Surface devices do not support daisy chaining, here is what you should do:

1. Use a Mini DisplayPort to DisplayPort cable, to connect to the Mini DisplayPort on your Surface to the DisplayPort input on the first monitor. And if only one of your monitors has an output port, you should connect your Surface to that monitor first.

2. Also, connect the output port of the first monitor to the DisplayPort input port of the second monitor.

3. Adhere strictly to the manufacturer's instructions to properly set up the two monitors to use DisplayPort 1.2 as an input source. For instance, this might be called Multi-Stream Transport (MST),

which helps the first monitor to pass the signal along to the second monitor.

If you have decided that your cables are the problem, move to **Solution 4.**

Solution 4: Check the display adapter

If you're using an adapter (such as Surface video adapter, USB-C to HDMI Adapter, USB-C to DisplayPort Adapter, or USB-C to VGA Adapter), check your connection and be sure it's fixed properly. You can disconnect the adapter and reinsert it firmly to ensure it is connected to your Surface.

Take Note: do not use a "Y" or "dual-link" adapter that will split the signal between two or more monitors.

In case you are using a Mini DisplayPort adapter, ensure the adapter is plugged in the right way. And also take note that the adapter will only work when the connector is plugged in with the flat side of the connector aligned with the flat side of the Mini DisplayPort.

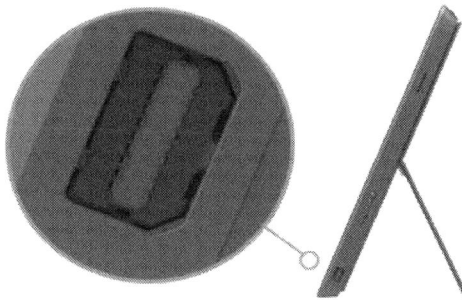

This is how a Mini DisplayPort looks. The Mini Display Port may be fixed in another place on your Surface or docking station.

In case your monitor does not support DisplayPort, I recommend you to use HDMI or you can use DVI or VGA. The following under-listed adapters have been tested for compatibility and can help solve video issues.

USB-C	Surface USB-C to DisplayPort Adapter for Business
	Surface USB-C to HDMI Adapter
	Surface USB-C to VGA Adapter
HDMI	Club3D Mini DisplayPort 1.2 to HDMI 2.0 Active Adapter (Model CAC-1170) - Active
	Surface Mini DisplayPort to HDMI 2.0 Adapter (Model 1819) - Active
DVI	Gofanco mDP to DVI Active Converter (Model mDPDVIA) - Active
	Cable Matters mDP-to-DVI (model 101022) - Active
	Note: For best results, use a DVI Dual Link Cable.
VGA	Microsoft Mini DisplayPort-to-VGA (model 1820) - Active

If you don't get the required result on your second screen, move on to **Solution 5.**

Solution 5 is to Clear your display cache

Take Note: These steps should not be used if you are running Windows 10 in S mode.

A few tips on how to clear your cache:

1. From the Surface Dock, undock your Surface or disconnect the monitor from your Surface.

2. Then download the Surface Dock registry file. After the download is complete, open the file. With this file your cache will be cleared, whether you have a dock or not.

3. Select and run **surface dock registry.reg.**

4. Click **Yes** to allow your Surface get the necessary changes, tap **Yes** to confirm, and then click on **OK** to close Surface.

5. You can restart your Surface, reconnect the Dock and/or monitors, and also try your external display again.

If you do not achieve results on your second screen, go on and try **Solution 6.**

Solution 6 is to Change the supported resolution and refresh rates

When you connect your Surface to a TV or monitor, the Surface will attempt to set the best resolution based on the connector and the resolution of your TV or monitor. You can change the settings to improve the quality of the video:

You have two options, either

- Change screen resolution or
- In Windows 10, Change the size of the text.

The resolution and refresh rate supported for the external display depends largely on how many displays are connected and whether the display on your Surface is on or off.

If after changing the resolution of your display and adjusting desktop sizes the issues persist, explore **Solution 7.**

Solution 7: Check your monitor's compatibility

There are different varieties of compatible monitors that you will find for your Surface.

But take note that these monitors aren't supported with Surface and Surface Dock

So they do have connection problems with Surface and Surface Dock. (You can contact the manufacturer for more help)

If your monitor is having issues with connecting to your Surface, check the firmware version that is installed on your monitor. Then visit your monitor manufacturer's website to know more on how to find your monitor's firmware version.

Some DisplayPort video issues can be fixed by disabling "MST mode" or "DP1.2 mode" on your monitor. You can also check the manual that came with your monitor to know how. By disabling "MST mode" or "DP1.2 mode" on your monitor, the display daisy-chaining will stop working. And if you're using more than one monitor, I recommend that you connect the two monitors directly to your Surface Dock, one to each Mini DisplayPort on your dock.

Adapter manufacturers at a later date, after August 28, 2018, that may be the cause of new issues unknown today.

The list is made available for you to make reference to it, and also to get necessary information too.

In no way is Microsoft giving you any guarantees or warranty that the monitors or adapters mentioned above will work properly with your Surface device, neither is Microsoft advising you to use any of the mentioned monitors or adapters in any manner.

Also take note that this list is not meant to be interpreted as a commitment from Microsoft, and Microsoft cannot give you guarantee of the correctness of any of the information given here. Microsoft gives no assurance, whether express, implied or statutory, as to the information on this page.

If you accept to use the list provided here, it is at your own risk and you agree to the fact that this list does not replace, add to, or change the terms of warranty that comes along with your Surface device. If you do not accept this terms, make sure you don't use this list.

In case you discover that your monitor is compatible, but you still require assistance, please move on to **Solution 8.**

Solution 8 is to Try the adapter on a different external display

For you to see that your video adapter is working, connect your Surface to another TV, monitor, or a projector. And if you cannot get what is on your Surface display to show on another external screen, the option is to replace the adapter.

Solution 9: Check out these possibilities if your display is wireless

Know that the models of Surface Studio, Surface Book, Surface Go, Surface Pro, Surface Laptop, and Surface 3 can all be connected wirelessly to compatible displays using Miracast by tapping on **Win+P** and choosing **Connect to a wireless display**. You can also connect your Surface without cables to an HDMI-compatible display this is done by using the Microsoft Wireless Display Adapter.

If to connect your Surface to a display wirelessly is giving you problems, I suggest you try the under-listed solutions in their order.

Be sure your display supports Miracast

For you to successfully connect your Surface to a display wirelessly without using the Microsoft Wireless Display Adapter, then know that the display must be a compatible one with Miracast. I recommend you to visit the manufacturer's website to know if your TV, monitor, or projector supports Miracast.

You can Restart your Surface and your TV, monitor, or projector

In some cases, simple restart can help you resolve the problems. Go to your Surface, and click on the Start button and then press Power > Update and restart. The TV or other display should be turned off and on, before you try connecting them again.

Install the latest updates

In most cases, when you download and install the recent updates for Windows and your Surface, the issues will be fixed. Go to Install Surface and Windows updates to know how.

Turn off Bluetooth on your Surface

Sometimes, Bluetooth can interfere with Miracast. So choose the action center Notification icon in the taskbar and turn your Bluetooth off.

Using the Microsoft Wireless Display Adapter with Surface

Share what is on your Surface screen with the use of a Microsoft Wireless Display Adapter. Stream videos, view photos, or show a presentation on a screen.

- Before you start
- Install the Microsoft Wireless Display Adapter App.
- Hook up with the adapter
- Modify the name of your adapter
- Use your TV, monitor, or projector as a secondary screen

Microsoft Wireless Display Adapter

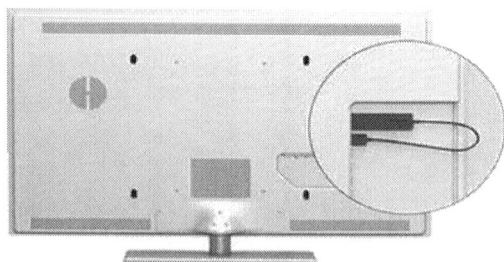

Microsoft Wireless Display Adapter plugged into an HDTV

Microsoft Wireless Display Adapter (With Microsoft Four Sq Logo)

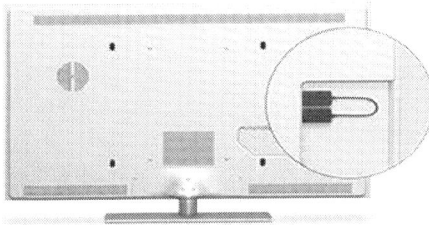

Before you start

A few things to understand before you start:

• You got to plug the Microsoft Wireless display adapter into a USB charging port, as this will gets power from the USB connection

• The adapter works best if you've both an HDMI port and a USB charging port on your HDTV, monitor, or projector.

• The device you are connecting to does not have a USB charging port. So, plug the USB end of the adapter into the USB charging port on a Surface professional power supply, a Surface moorage station, or any other USB charger.

• If your Surface is running on Windows 8, it would be best to upgrade to Windows 8.1 or Windows 10 before using the Microsoft Wireless display adapter.

Install the Microsoft Wireless Display Adapter application

Prior to connecting your Surface to the adapter, ensure you install the Microsoft Wireless Display Adapter App from the Microsoft Store:

1. Go to **Start,** and select **All Apps > Microsoft Store.**

2. Ensure you're logged in with your Microsoft account.

3. Within the search box, enter **Microsoft Wireless Display Adapter.**

4. Choose the title for the App, and choose **Free.** The application will install on your Surface.

Connect With the Adapter

1. Fit in the HDMI end of the adapter into the HDMI port on your HDTV, screen, or projector.

2. Fit in the USB end of the adapter into a USB charging port on your HDTV, screen, or projector.

3. On your HDTV, screen, or projector, set the input to HDMI.

4. On your Surface, swipe in from the right edge of the screen, or select **action center Notification symbol** within the taskbar.

5.Choose **Connect**, and in the display list, select the name of the Microsoft Wireless Display Adapter.

Rename Your Adapter

1. Go to **Start** , and select **All Apps > Microsoft Wireless Display Adapter.**

2. Below **Adapter settings**, choose the name of the adapter

If the name seems dim, the adapter settings may be bolted. At the base of the screen, select Create password, and adhere to the on-screen guidelines.

3. Enter another name for your adapter, and press Enter.

The new name will produce results quickly, yet to see it on your Surface, you'll have to disconnect and reconnect the adapter

Here's how to do it:

1. Swipe in from the right edge of the screen, or **select action center Notification symbol** in the taskbar.

2. Select **Connect**, choose the name of the Microsoft Wireless Display Adapter, and select **Disconnect**.

3. To reconnect, swipe in from the right edge of the screen, select **Connect**, and in the display list, choose the name of the adapter.

Keep Others from Connecting With Your Adapter

To keep others from pairing with or utilizing your adapter without your authorization, you can change the pairing mode to Require a PIN code to pair. Here's the means by which to enable this setting:

1. Go to **Start**, and select All **Apps** > **Microsoft Wireless Display Adapter**.

2. Below **Pairing mode**, select **Requires PIN code to pair**.

Windows recollects connected devices, so the adapter won't prompt you to enter a PIN in the event that you connect with it using the same Surface.

In the event that you attempt to connect with the adapter utilizing another device, your HDTV, screen, or projector will show an arbitrarily created PIN. Fill in the PIN in the Microsoft Wireless Display Adapter application on your Surface, and choose **Next** to connect.

Utilize Your HDTV, Screen, or Projector As A Secondary Screen

After you have connected your Surface to the adapter, you can use your HDTV, screen, or projector as a secondary screen. You can stream videos wirelessly to your connected device over your home network, or from your preferred video streaming services.

You can likewise move apps between your Surface and your connected device, or utilize at least two applications next to each other.

Troubleshooting Wireless Display Adapters

If you run into problems with a wireless display adapter, here are some troubleshooting steps to help settle them.

Before you start

Plug the adapter into a HDMI port on your HDTV, screen, or projector and into a USB charging port. The adapter gets its power from the USB charging port.

To get the best result, keep your device within 23 feet of the HDTV, projector, or screen.

The adapter can connect with just a single HDTV, screen, or projector at once.

Use the Microsoft Wireless Display Adapter application to update the firmware.

Experiencing Difficulty Connecting Your Device To The Adapter?

In case you're experiencing difficulty connecting your device to the Microsoft Wireless Display Adapter, attempt these solutions all together.

Solution 1: Install the most recent updates

Installing the most recent updates for your device and Windows can help fix numerous basic associated issues. For Windows devices, here's how to do it:

1. Select **Start** > **Settings** > **Update and security** > **Windows Update**.

2. Select Check for updates. In the event that updates are accessible, they will install consequently. You may need to restart your device after the updates have been installed.

If installing updates doesn't help, attempt Solution 2.

Solution 2: Check your HDMI and USB connections

Ensure both the HDMI end and USB end of the connector are connected accurately.

• Ensure the HDMI end of the adapter is connected with the HDMI port on your HDTV, screen, or projector. Use the enclosed HDMI extension cable if necessary.

• Ensure the USB end of the adapter is connected to a USB power source.

Notes

• If the HDTV, screen, or projector you're connecting with doesn't have a USB charging port, you can use the USB charging port on a device power supply or some other USB charger.

• Use a USB cord if you need more length for your USB connector.

• Make sure the electrical outlet you're utilizing for USB power is functioning properly. Test it by connecting something different.

In case you're still experiencing difficulty despite everything, attempt Solution 3.

Solution 3: Restart the adapter

1. Take away the Microsoft Wireless Display Adapter from the TV or screen.

2. Restart your device.

3. Re-embed the Microsoft Wireless Display adapter into your TV or screen.

4. Attempt to display once again.

Note

We prescribed you check for updates on both your device, and Microsoft Wireless Display Adapter when you finish Solution 3.

In the event that despite everything you have a haul, attempt Solution 4.

Solution 4: Reset the adapter

Take a step at resetting the adapter. This is often useful if you have forgotten your password. Here's how to do it:

1. On the adapter beside the wired connection, press and hold the reset button for 10 seconds. The LED light on the adapter will blink.

2. At the point when the message "Ready to connect" shows up on your secondary screen, swipe in from the right edge of your device screen or choose **Action Center** within the taskbar.

3. Select **Connect**, and in the display list, choose the name of the Microsoft Wireless Display Adapter.

If resetting the adapter doesn't take care of the issue, attempt Solution 5.

Solution 5: Remove the adapter and reconnect

There may be an issue with the connection between your device and the adapter. To fix the issue, take a step at disengaging the adapter from your device and reconnecting it. Here's how:

1. Select **Start** > **Settings** > **Devices** > **Connected gadgets**.

2. Below Projectors, choose the name of the Microsoft Wireless Display Adapter and select Remove device

3. Select **Add a device** to connect your gadget and the Microsoft Wireless Display Adapter.

In the event that disconnecting and reconnecting the adapter doesn't help, attempt Solution 6.

Solution 6: Allow the adapter to speak through Windows Firewall

Windows Firewall may be keeping the adapter from connecting with your device. To enable the adapter to speak through the firewall:

1. Within the search enclosed in the taskbar, type **allow firewall**, and within the search result, select **Allow an application through Windows Firewall**.

2. Below **Name**, find **Wireless Display** and ensure **Private** and **Public** are chosen. Next, select **OK**.

Note: If you can't choose anything in the **Allowed applications** and **features** box, you aren't signed in as an administrator. Select **Change Settings**, type your password, and afterward select **Yes**. Your password should be the same to the password you used to set up your device.

Next, ensure **Private** and **Public** are chosen and afterward select **OK**.

If your firewall is set to enable the adapter to speak and you still can't connect, attempt Solution 7.

Solution 7: Amend the wireless frequency band on your device

The Microsoft Wireless Display Adapter can speak with a device on either the 2.4GHz or 5GHz wireless frequency bands. However, you should have the 2.4GHz band authorized on your device when you're pairing your device with the adapter.

In case despite everything you're experiencing difficulty connecting your device to the adapter, the 2.4GHz band may be disabled.

Here's the way to modify the 2.4 GHz, or 5 GHz band:

1. Select the search enclosed in the taskbar, type **device manager**, and in the search results, choose **Device Manager**.

2. Select the arrow next to **Network adapters**, then press and hold (or right-click) your device's network adapter.

Select **Properties** > **Advanced**. If you don't see the **Advanced** tab, you're not logged in as associate administrator. Select **Change Settings**, enter your password, and select **Yes**. Your password ought to be equivalent to the password you used to set up your device. Next, select **Advanced**.

3. Below Property, select **Band**.

4. Below **Value**, select the arrow and choose Auto > **OK**.

If regardless you can't connect, attempt Solution 8.

Solution 8: Reinstall the Intel HD Graphics driver

An issue with the Intel HD Graphics driver on your gadget may be keeping your device from speaking with the Microsoft Wireless Display Adapter. Take a step at uninstalling and reinstalling the driver. Here's how to do it:

1. Select the search enclosed in the taskbar, type **device manager**, and within the search result, select **Device Manager**.

2. Select the arrow beside **Display adapter**, at that point press and hold (or right-click) the Intel HD Graphics driver.

3. Select **Uninstall**.

4. Select **Start** > **Power** > **Restart**.

5. After your device restarts, select Start > **Settings** > **Devices** > **Connected devices**.

6. Choose **Add a device** to connect your device and the Microsoft Wireless Display Adapter.

If despite everything you can't connect your device to your Microsoft Wireless Display Adapter, attempt solution 9.

Solution 9: Uninstall and Reinstall the device Wi-Fi driver

1. In the search box on the taskbar, type **device manager**, and afterward select **Device Manager** from the results.

2. Select the arrow by **Network adapters**, then press and hold (or right-click) your device's network adapter.

3. Select **Uninstall**.

4. Select **Start** > **Power** > **Restart**.

5. After your gadget restarts, select **Start** > **Settings** > **Devices** > **Connected devices**.

6. Choose **Add a device** to connect your device and the Microsoft Wireless Display Adapter.

If you are still having issues connecting your device to your Microsoft Wireless Display Adapter, then contact Microsoft Support.

Experiencing Difficulty with Video or Sound Playback?

If you've got any of these issues with video or sound playback, here are a few solutions to attempt:

Nothing shows on the secondary screen

In the event that you have connected your device to the adapter and nothing shows on your secondary screen, attempt these solutions:

• Ensure your device is set to copy or expand the screen.

• Unplug the USB end of the connector to turn it off, and plug it back to turn it on once more.

• Ensure your HDTV, screen, or projector is set to the HDMI channel.

• Ensure your HDTV, screen, or projector supports HDCP. If you aren't sure if your display supports HDCP, check the information that accompanied your device or go to the manufacturer's website.

• Make sure your HDTV, screen, or projector supports HDCP. On the off chance that you aren't sure if your TV supports HDCP, check the information that accompanied your device or go to the manufacturer's website.

Video Is Pixelated Or Sound Stutters

If you discover pixelation in the video or if the sound stutters, attempt the following:

• Move your gadget closer to the adapter. For best execution, your gadget ought to be within 23 feet of your HDTV, screen, or projector.

• Move the adapter away from microwaves, cordless telephones, or baby monitors. Basic household electronics like these can cause radio recurrence impedance that may upset the connection between your device and the adapter.

• If you need more space to connect the adapter to the HDMI port on your secondary screen, use the HDMI extension cable that was enclosed in the container your adapter came in. If you've plugged the adapter into the HDMI port at an angle, this will cause problems with the video quality

Apps based video (YouTube, Netflix, Amazon) can't play while connected with the Wireless Display Adapter

In case you're having issues playing video and content from an application service like Netflix, YouTube, or Amazon Instant Video, attempt the underneath steps:

1. Ensure the connector is modern.

2. Close and relaunch, or refresh the application.

3. Remove the Wireless Display Adapter.

4. Restart the device.

5. Reconnect to the adapter and play the video once more.

Video Plays on Your Device However Is Static On Your Secondary Screen

If videos normally plays effectively on your gadget but now are static on your screen, remove the adapter from your device and the display, and reconnect it. Here's how to do it:

1. Swipe in from the right edge of the screen or choose the action focus Notification symbol in the taskbar.

2. Choose **Connect**, and select the name of the Microsoft Wireless Display Adapter, and choose **Disconnect**.

3. Unplug the two ends of the adapter from your HDTV, screen, or projector and plug them in once more.

4. Swipe in from the right edge of the screen or choose the action center Notification symbol in the taskbar.

5. Select Connect, and in the display list, select the name of the Microsoft Wireless Display Adapter to reconnect your device to the adapter.

Poor Video Quality

If the standard of the streaming video is poor, here are a few different ways to help improve it:

• Ensure you're not using a HDMI to VGA converter. Changing over from HDMI to VGA reduces the signal quality of the video output and can distort the pictures.

• Reduce recurrent impedance by moving the adapter away from microwaves, cordless telephones, and other basic family unit hardware.

• Move your device closer to the adapter. The adapter works its best when it's within 23 feet of your device

• Download best-quality video. The source itself may be of low quality, which will influence the nature of the streaming video.

Video plays on the connected display, however sound comes from your device

1. The search box on the taskbar, type sound, and afterward select Sound from the outcomes.

2. Choose **Playback** > **Speakers/Intel WiDi** > **Set Default** > **OK.**

Can't Modify the Resolution On Your Device

In the event that the resolution on your HDTV, screen, or projector is under 1080p, your gadget will default to that resolution while it's connected with the display.

You need a HDTV, screen, or projector that supports up to 1080p to stream content from your device in that resolution. After you detach your device from the adapter, your device will return to its default resolution.

Display isn't to scale, or a few pieces of the display are absent?

If part of the screen on your device doesn't show up on your secondary screen, the display probably won't be to scale. Attempt these solutions:

Adjust the Resolution on Your Device

If you set the resolution on your device to a lower resolution than its default setting, increase the resolution to fit effectively on your second screen. Here's how to do it:

1. In the search box on the taskbar, type screen resolution, then select **Change the screen resolution** from the results.

2. Below **Resolution**, select the arrow and afterward select the resolution that is **Recommended**. (The highest resolution is the suggested resolution on the device.)

3. Choose **Apply**.

Use the Microsoft Wireless Display Adapter Apps To Change Display Settings

You can use the adapter application to change how the screen on your device scales to the screen on your HDTV, screen, or projector. Here's how to do it:

1. Open the Microsoft Wireless Display Adapter application.

2. Below **Adjust display**, drag the slider to one side until you can see everything that is on your device on the HDTV, screen, or projector.

Experiencing difficulty with the Microsoft Wireless Display Adapter application?

In case you're having issues with the Microsoft Wireless Display Adapter application, here are a few things to attempt.

The application shows "You're not connected"

If the message "You're not connected" shows up in the application:

1. Ensure both the HDMI end and the USB end of the connector are connected with your HDTV, screen, or projector.

2. In the App, select **Refresh.**

Application Consistently Shows "Waiting For Connection"

Note

The adapter won't work in case you're using a proxy server to access the web. If the app consistently shows "**Waiting for connection**" first ensure your device is connected with the adapter, at that point disconnect the adapter and reconnect it. Here's how to do it:

1. Swipe in from the right edge of the screen or choose **Action Center Notification symbol** in the taskbar.

2. Select **Connect.** The adapter will show up at the top of the menu. (If the adapter doesn't show up at the top, your device isn't connected with the adapter.)

3. Choose the name of the Microsoft Wireless Display Adapter and select **Disconnect**.

4. Swipe in from the right edge of the screen or choose **Action Center Notification symbol** in the taskbar .

5. Select **Connect**, and from the display, choose the name of the Microsoft Wireless Display Adapter to reconnect your device to the adapter.

Note

The adapter won't work if you are using a proxy server to access to the web.

How to Set Up LTE Connection for Microsoft Surface Pro

Remain connected to the internet after you've completed your LTE set up.

You can only get mobile data on your device using two methods;

1. By obtaining a Nano-SIM from your mobile operator and subscribing for a data plan.

2. By using the eSIM provided by Surface Pro: The integrated SIM comes with Windows 10 Mobile Plan Application. From the application, you will be required to sign up as a new user or add your device to your former account.

How to use your mobile operator's data plans after obtaining a Nano-SIM

1. Subscribe for a broadband connection or renew your subscription by getting in touch with your mobile operator.

2. Surface Pro has a place for inserting your Nano-SIM. To do this, head to "Insert a SIM into your Surface."

3. After inserting your SIM, Click on "Start" and follow the order below:

- "Settings"
- **"Network & Internet"**
- **"Cellular"**
- **"Use this SIM," then select SIM1 to complete the setup.**

How to use the Mobile Plans Application from the Microsoft Surface eSIM

It is essential to get a Wi-Fi connection before opening the Mobile Plans application as a new user.

However, you can add a new device to your old account. The only requirement necessary is the installation of the 1803 version of Windows 10 (you can also do this for a higher Win10 version). To get updates, click on Start and follow the order below:

- "Settings"
- "Update & security"
- "Windows Update"
- "Check for updates."

How to Switch between Nano-SIM data and eSIM data

You can change from Nano-SIM to eSIM or vice versa if you have set up the two on your phone. Do this by, clicking "Start" and follow the process;

- Go to "Settings"
- "Network & Internet"
- "Cellular"
- Use this SIM for cellular data
- For data plan from your phone operator using the Nano-SIM, click on SIM 1
- For Mobile data application using the eSIM, click on eSIM

You can only get mobile data on your device using two methods;

1. By obtaining a Nano-SIM from your mobile operator and subscribing for a data plan.

2. By using the eSIM provided by Microsoft Surface Pro. The integrated SIM comes with Windows 10 Mobile Plan Application.

3. From the application, you will be required to sign up as a new user or add your device to your former account.

How to use your mobile operator's data plans after obtaining a Nano-SIM

1. Subscribe for a broadband connection or renew your subscription by getting in touch with your mobile operator.

2. The Surface Pro has a place for inserting your Nano-SIM.

3. After inserting your SIM, Click on "Start" and follow the order below:

   - "Settings"
   - "Network & Internet"
   - "Cellular"
   - "Use this SIM," then select SIM1 to complete the setup.

How to use the Mobile Plans Application from the eSIM in Surface Pro with LTE advanced

It is essential to get a Wi-Fi connection before opening the Mobile Plans application as a new user.

However, you can add a new device to your old account. The only requirement necessary is the installation of the 1803 version of Windows 10 (you can also do this for a higher Win10 version). To get updates, click on Start and follow the order below:

- "Settings"
- "Update & security"
- "Windows Update"
- "Check for updates."

How to Switch between Nano-SIM data and eSIM data

You can change from Nano-SIM to eSIM or vice versa if you have set up the two on your phone. Do this by clicking "Start" and follow the process;

- Go to "Settings"
- "Network & Internet"
- "Cellular"
- Use this SIM for cellular data
- For data plan from your phone operator using the Nano-SIM, click on SIM 1
- For Mobile data application using the eSIM, click on eSIM

How can I switch from Nano-SIM data to eSIM data

It is possible to have Nano-SIM and eSIM data plans on your Surface device; it is also easy to change between the data plans. To do this, click "Start" and follow the process;

- Go to "Settings"
- "Network & Internet"
- "Cellular"
- Use this SIM for cellular data
- For data plan from your phone operator using the Nano-SIM, click on SIM 1
- For Mobile data application using the eSIM, click on eSIM

Note that you can only open the Mobile Plans Application with a Wi-Fi connection if you are setting up your eSIM as a new user.

How will I get mobile data on my Surface Pro with LTE Advanced?

There are just two methods, which are as follows:

1. By obtaining a Nano-SIM from your mobile operator and subscribing for a data plan.
2. By using the eSIM provided by Surface Pro with LTE Advanced: The integrated SIM comes with Windows 10 Mobile Plan Application. From the application, you will be required to

sign up as a new user or add your device to your former account.

Is It Possible To Change From Mobile Data To A Non-Metered Network?

Yes, it is. When a good and unsuspicious non-metered network like the Wi-Fi is available, it is advisable to use in place of the mobile data. This is because Wi-Fi is sometimes free or cheaper than data plans.

How Can I Avoid Unnecessary Waste Of My Data?

Converse with your network provider to find out which data package is best for you; not everyone uses the same size of data. It indeed relies upon how you utilize your gadget, how frequently, and location.

Here are a few interesting points:

Try a Wi-Fi connection: in a situation where your data package is limited, you can use a trusted Wi-Fi connection if it is available. Wi-Fi is regularly more affordable than using the data plan from your mobile operator.

Set your device to utilize metering when using data packages: This can assist you with decreasing the measure of data you use by constraining the extent of updates, stopping downloads, not refreshing the tiles in the Start menu, and confining different things that send and get information.

To see whether your mobile data is set as metered, go to Start and select "Settings." Pick "Network and Internet" > "Cellular" > "Advanced options." From the advanced options, you will see "Set as a metered connection" under the metered connection.

On the Advanced alternatives screen for your cell information association, take a gander at the Set as a metered association setting under Metered association.

Monitor your evaluated use of data: There is an application for monitoring how you use data. Your mobile operator provides the app, or you can monitor it from the Windows network setup.

1. Click on "Start" and go to Settings. Select "Network & Internet" > "Data Usage."

2. In the event that you purchased a prepaid data package from a service provider through the Mobile Plans application, you should check your data balance from the taskbar. From the taskbar, click "Network" and you will see the balance under the name of the network you use.

3. When using metered connections, reduce your syncing: For instance, you can do this for OneDrive app so that you only sync when uploading or downloading to the app.

4. Switch off OneDrive syncing from the settings. For instance, in your settings for OneDrive, turn off adjusting over metered associations. Empower matching up just when you have to transfer or download to OneDrive.

5. To figure out which applications should sync with your data plan, go to Settings from the "Start" tab. Select "Network & Internet" > "Cellular" and pick the apps you want for your data.

Switching your email download options to manual saves data than being automatic.

Restrict data-intensive tasks: You consume more data when you share data during games; use applications that stream data like video streaming, or use your device for Wi-Fi hotspot.

Use your phone operator's applications: several phone companies provide users with apps that you can use to check account information, use of data e.t.c.

In most cases, the installation of such applications during setup is automatic. You can visit the online store of your phone operators for apps or visit the Windows store.

If you want to check any installed app from your network provider;

1. Choose Start, go to "Settings" > "Network & Internet" > "Cellular"

2. From the list shown under "Cellular," select the network. Once you see "View My Account," it is an indication that you have downloaded an application from your phone operator.

I will be leaving my current country, is it necessary to modify the configurations on my Microsoft Surface?

In a situation where you already have a subscription with your network provider, it is best to get in touch with them to find out about their international subscription to alleviate cost concerns when traveling. Another option is to find out if you can purchase a prepaid SIM card and data plan in the region you are traveling to.

The eSIM Mobile Plans Application allows you to buy a data package from any network provider in any location. However, this depends on the availability of data from the providers in that location.

It is best to adjust some settings on your device, so you don't incur unnecessary data fees. For instance, when you are in a location that is not supported by your network provider, it is advisable to disable roaming.

Another useful tip is to use a Wi-Fi connection instead of data when you are traveling. This will help you cut down unnecessary data costs.

I purchased this particular Microsoft Surface for data use, is it a must to configure it with Wi-Fi?

You have to use a Wi-Fi connection to set up your eSIM as a new user.

From your Mobile Plans Application, subscribe for a data package by purchasing from your network provider. Keep in mind that you need an active account for your eSIM connection.

I Find It Difficult To Connect Even When My SIM Is In The Surface Device, What Am I Missing?

Check out the possible reasons below:

- It may be that Windows updates are outdated and needs upgrading.
- You may have stepped out of the coverage range of your network provider.
- You may have exhausted your data subscription.
- You should also ensure that the APN (Access Point Name) is picked up by your network provider.

You may have chosen "Let Windows manage this connection," which will disable your data when using a Wi-Fi connection or wired ethernet connection. Find out if this option is switched on by clicking "Start." Go to "Settings" > Network & Internet > Cellular. You would find it hard to connect until you deactivate other networks first.

You can surf the net in different locations with the help of a cellular signal. Some Microsoft devices with Windows 10 are built for this, with the Nano-SIM and eSIM available. However, if your device does not have any of the SIM options (Nano or eSIM), An alternative way to connect to the internet is by inserting a modem or wireless broadband system. However, this does not eliminate the fact that you still need a data plan for a connection.

Setting Up Your Connection As A New User

1. Click on the icon at the bottom corner on the right of the taskbar. This takes you to the Network options where you will pick the mobile network icon that emerges in the display. In most cases, besides the mobile network logo, you will see the label of your network provider.

2. Click "Connect" if "Let Windows Keep me connected" is unchecked.   If the box is checked, connections to the mobile data will be automatic. Ensure you are not already connected to Wi-Fi or any shared network.

3. Fill in details like username, password, and APN (Access Point Name) when a prompt shows up.

If you need to, you can search for more information on what configuration to use with your Windows 10 phone, SIM card, or mobile network.

Note if you see "Mobile Operator Locked" under the name of your service provider, it means that you need to properly insert the SIM card of your phone company for connection.

Switch the "Cellular Quick Action" on if you notice that it is switched off. To do this, tap the Network icon from the taskbar. When such an option is switched off, there is no way you can connect to your network provider because the cellular radio is off.

How to Use Cellular Data Settings When Having Issues with Connection

In the event that your connection is working smoothly, you may not need this. If you have difficulties with data connections, however, it will become necessary to change one or more configurations.

Here is a list of the mobile configurations you should try out to eliminate issues with cellular connections. These settings differ from one model to another and the service provider, which is unique to a location.:

1. The "Let Windows Manage This Connection" Option

This option decides whether your Windows 10 gadget will be connected automatically to the mobile data anytime it is available. Make sure the mobile connection box is unchecked every time you decide to make a manual connection. Nevertheless, you should check it for an automatic connection where Windows perform the connection on its own. Provided you are not on Wi-Fi or Ethernet connection; the mobile data connection will be automatic if you check the box.

2. **To access the** "Let **Windows manage this connection" option**: From the "Start" option, go to "Settings" > "Network & Internet" > "Cellular." You can get this configuration when you are not connected to the mobile network. However, when you tap "Connect," the setting is applied.

3. The "Use this SIM for cellular data" option

You can pick the SIM you will use for a data connection from this option. If you are concerned about data costs, this is where you will pick a suitable SIM for mobile connection. Simply select the SIM that is more cost-effective.

To access "Use this SIM for cellular data," go to the device settings from the "Start" option. From there, Select "Network & Internet" > "Cellular," and it will be displayed for you.

4. Data Roaming Options

This option decides if data is switched on or off when you are beyond the coverage of your network operator. You can help avoid data roaming fees by choosing "Don't roam."

If you enable data roaming, your data will be active even when your Surface device is in a roaming zone, You may be charged for more for the data used when roaming, but this depends on if your subscription is still available.

To access Data roaming:

1. Go to the Surface settings by tapping the "Start" option. From here, pick "Network & Internet" > "Cellular," and the option will be displayed.

2. Select Mobile data rather than Wi-Fi connection

You might consider mobile data if you are in a situation where the Wi-Fi connection is slow or if you are in a location where your mobile data connection is strong (faster).

For situations like this, if you pick the "When Wi-Fi is poor or Always" option, your device will automatically use the best service depending on the area. When using mobile data, data from your subscription will be used, and costs may be incurred.

Click the Start option to find this feature, then select "Settings" > "Network & Internet" > "Cellular."

5. Pick applications that can utilize your mobile data

If you want to control the amount of data used, you can pick which applications can or can't utilize mobile data. For instance, in the case of an application that uses a great deal of data even when you don't utilize it regularly, you probably won't need that application to use more data.

To get to this setting, pick the "Start" button and go to the Settings. Select "Network and Internet" > "Cellular" > Choose applications that can utilize your cell information. On the screen displayed, do at least one of these:

6. Turn off "Let apps use my cellular data" for unwanted applications.

Applications won't be permitted to utilize your mobile data. However, the applications will be active when you are using Wi-Fi or an Ethernet connection.

Look for the application under "Choose apps that can use your cellular data," and afterward turn off mobile data for that unwanted app.

7. Picking a Network

This option shows up while roaming and decides which network is utilized for data connection: without prior setting, this is automatic.

If you attempt to use a mobile connection and get a notification that your preferred network is not available, you can pick "Search for networks," and afterward pick another mobile connection.

To discover this configuration, tap the "Start" option, afterward select "Settings." From here, pick "Network and Internet" > "Cellular" > "Advanced options."

8. Active Network

This option showcases the name of the mobile network that you're utilizing.

You can discover this setting by tapping the "Start" button; at that point, choose "Settings" > "Network and Internet" > "Cellular" > "Advanced choices."

9. Set as a metered connection

With a metered connection, you can surf the web when you have data plans, but there is a limit to it. Mobile data connections are automatically set to be metered. Many applications function on a metered connection in different ways so that the amount of data used is conserved. With a metered connection, most updates for your Surface device are done manually.

When you have a data allowance for your mobile data in Data Usage Settings, the device will help you maintain that data limit and adjust the settings for you. To see this option tap the "Start" button. From here, go to "Settings" > "Network & Internet" > "Cellular" > Advanced options.

10. Add an APN

The name of the internet address that your device use in connection to the web is known as the Access Point Name (APN). APN is important for a mobile data connection. Normally, the APN setting is configured by default.

If you find that your device connection is not functioning and you can't surf the net, input a new Internet APN, which you will get from your network provider in your area. If you find it impossible to connect to a Wi-Fi channel on your device, use another phone to search the web for APN settings for your network provider.

1. Choose the "Start" button, then choose "Settings" > "Network & Internet" > "Cellular" > "Advanced Options" > Add APN.

2. After this, you can try to:

• Type in the APN profile name in the profile name slot

• Type in the APN address in the APN slot

• Type in the username for your device in the username slot

• Type in the password in the password slot

• Pick the type of sign-in information and choose the authentication method to use

• Pick the type of IP and IP address to use

• Pick the type of APN and choose the "Internet."

1. Then Check the box beside the "Apply this profile" option. This will make the profile available for use once you save it.

2. Tap "Save" and "OK"

3. If you want to check all the saved APN profiles, tap "Back," and you will find them under the "Internet Option" option.

11. Properties

This option shows you all you need to know about your Mobile connection and SIM. Under this option, you will get your IMEI (International Mobile Equipment Identity) number.

If you want to copy any information here, click "Copy." Copying the information becomes necessary when you want to inform the phone company about any issues you are having with the connection.

You can get this option when you go to the "Settings" after selecting "Start." From the Settings, choose "Network & Internet > "Cellular" and "Advanced options."

12. Use SIM PIN

This option is important if you want to use a PIN for the SIM in your window 10 device so that others won't use the cellular data connection when you're not authorized. Then you'll be encouraged to type the SIM PIN after setting up SIM PIN.

You need to type your SIM PIN when encouraged. And if you're doing this for the first time, you'll have to type the default SIM PIN. You'll be forced to visit your mobile operator's website in order to know if the list is there, just in case you don't know the default SIM PIN. To lock your cellular data connection with a SIM PIN, you'll need to restart your Windows 10 device.

Type your SIM PIN when requested, then you click OK; when you have your PIN for your SIM already fixed up.

In order to get the SIM PIN setting done, you'll need to select the start button, then select settings, then Network & internet , Cellular, Advanced option, Then Use SIM PIN under the security section.

13. Remove the SIM PIN

When you're using a SIM PIN, "Remove the SIM PIN" automatically pops up. In the case whereby you don't want to use a SIM PIN that you've been using before, pick "Remove SIM PIN," input the SIM PIN you are using now, and then click "OK."

You choose the "Start button" and then go to settings. From here click "Network & Internet" > "Cellular" > "Advanced options." Then you click "Remove SIM PIN" under the security section.

14. Change SIM PIN

Change SIM PIN also appears if you're using a SIM PIN. When you're using a SIM PIN, and it needs to be changed; you select the 'change SIM PIN" button, then you type the current PIN you intend using in the "current SIM PIN" box, then you type a new SIM PIN in the "NEW SIM PIN" box, then type the same new SIM PIN in the "Confirm new SIM PIN" box then you click OK.

In order to find the " Change SIM PIN" settings; you click the **"Start" button," you then select "Settings," "Network & Internet,"** "Cellular," "Advanced options," then click "Change SIM PIN" in the security section

15. Unblock SIM PIN

"Unblock SIM PIN" pops up when you're using a SIM PIN, and you enter the incorrect pin trice. The SIM will automatically get blocked, and you'll be restricted from using it; if the incorrect PIN has been entered three times.Then you'll need to contact your mobile operator for the PUK code (PIN unblocking key).

Then you select the "Unblock SIM PIN." You then type the PIN Unblocking key (PUK) thereafter. Then, note that your SIM will be permanently blocked when you enter an incorrect PUK code is entered too many times.

Then, you'll be forced to get a new SIM card from the mobile operator. Now, you'll select the "Start button," then the "select button," "Network & Internet," "Cellular," "Advanced options," then you click the "Unblock SIM PIN" beneath the security section.Use the eSIM to get access to connection on your device.

Esim helps connect to the internet with a cellular data connection. You tend to avoid getting a SIM card from your mobile operator.

And you have the opportunity to switch between data plans and mobile operators. For instance, you tend to get connected quickly in more places, with the help of finding a mobile operator with plans in the area. This happens when you have one cellular data for work. And also, having a different plan with another mobile operator for personal use is involved.

What's needed to be done is:

You'll need a sound Windows 10 PC with version 1703 or the advanced version. Then you select the "Start button," you select "settings," "System," then "About"; in order to see the version of Windows 10 your device uses.

The two ways to know if your PC has an eSIM are:

- You select the "Start button," and then click select settings, Network & internet, Cellular.

- You look for a link near the bottom of the page that says "manageeSIM profiles" on the PC screen. Then if you see the link appear, definitely your PC has an eSIM.

Note: In case you don't see "Manage eSIM profile," but you see "Use this SIM for cellular data" at the upper part of the device, you'll need to choose it from the drop-down box. Ideally, this happens because some devices have both eSIM and Physical SIM card.

To Add an Esim Profile

In order to get internet connections using cellular data, you'll need to add an eSIM profile. It's most likely you have an eSIM profile already added to your PC if you have a PC from your organization. If you see an eSIM profile for a mobile operator, you expect to find when you select "Manage eSIM profiles"; this procedure can be skipped. Then go to the next one to get connected.

1.You select the "Start button," and then select settings, Network & Internet, Cellular, then "Manage eSIM profiles."

2. Then under eSIM profiles, you select Add a new profile.

3. To search for available profiles or in order to use an activation code you have from your mobile operator, you need to do the followings:

- Search for available profiles
- Select Search for available profiles > Next.
- Then when a profile you want to use is found, you click "Download."
- The confirmation code from your mobile operator needs to be entered in the corresponding box, and then you click download.
- After the profile must have been downloaded and installed, you then select "Continue" in order to find profiles you might want and then repeat the previous steps.
- Then you select "Close" when you must have downloaded the profiles you want.
- Make use of an activation code you have from your mobile operator
- Select your preferred PC camera, if you have a QR code to scan for the activation code, and then scan the QR code.
- Then you click "Next" when the activation code appears in the corresponding Activation code box.
- Then enter the confirmation code from your mobile operator into the corresponding box and then select "Download." This is to be done in the dialog box that asks, "Do you want to download this profile?".

- Afterward, you then select "Close."

4. Optional: You have to select the "profile," select "Edit name," "type a name you'll remember," and then select "save." This is to be done in order to give the profile a friendly name to help you remember it (For instance, Work or personal).

If you wish to make an eSIM connection, you need to:
- Select the "Start button", select "Settings", "Network & Internet", "Cellular", then "Manage eSIM profiles".
- Where eSIM profile is; you select the profile you want, and then select "Use."

3. You then select "Yes" for this will use cellular data from your data plan and may require charges.

Do you want to continue?

Then you'll automatically be connected to a cellular data network, and then you'll be opportune to use it.

To switch between profiles

You can switch between profile to use a different mobile operator and data plan in a situation where there are other profiles available.

1. go to the "Settings" from the "Start" option. "Network & Internet," "Cellular," "Manage eSIM profiles.

2. Select the profile you intend to stop using, and then select "Stop using." This is to be done under eSIM profiles.

3. You'll be disconnected from the cellular network when you click (Yes). Continue?

4. You then click (Use) after you've selected the different profiles you want to use.

To Delete a Profile

You can delete a profile from your PC, in case you don't want to use it anymore.Then you'll need to download the profile again and might need to contract your mobile operator if you delete the profile, and you intend adding it later on.

1. Click the "Select button," then click "Settings," Network & Internet, Cellular, and manage eSIM profiles.

2. Click the profile to delete, and then you click "Delete." This is to be done under "eSIM profiles."

3. Then you click "Yes" at the point whereby you wane that the profile will be permanently deleted.

Note: You might be restricted from deleting an eSIM profile if you have a PC from your organization because of a policy that is fit by your organization.

Insert a SIM card into your Surface

You'll need a nano SIM from your mobile carrier when you get a cellular data connection on your Surface Pro before you get started.

1. with your Surface Pro facing down, you carefully pull out of the kickstand. The kickstand has the Microsoft logo on the back.

2. Remove the SIM ejector device from the instruction card that's on top of the package your Surface Pro came in.

3. Locate your SIM card tray with LTE Advanced close to the bottom-right corner and under your Surface Pro kickstand.

4. Insert the SIM ejector device into the small hole and press the SIM card tray gently to eject. Slide the SIM ejector device back into the instruction card when you're finished so that you can locate it later.

5. Remove from the slot the SIM card tray. Leave it to face up when you remove it

6. Place the face-up SIM card on the SIM card tray. Be certain of the notch in the SIM card corner matches the one in the SIM card tray to fit properly.

The SIM card's words or logo should be faced-up.

7. Slide back the SIM card tray into the slot of your SIM card until it clicks. The small hole should be closest to the bottom-right corner in the SIM card tray. Make sure that the slides of the SIM card tray are smooth — do not force it.

The Device won't Switch on

You can try a couple of things to get your Surface pro to get it working again in the case whereby your surface won't turn on, wont wake up, or it is blank and not displaying the logo of Microsoft Surface.

Make sure your surface is charged after you must have disconnected accessories.

1. Disconnect any USB drives, SD cards, USB accessories, external monitors, docks, etc. that you have connected to your surface. So try to turn it on. If that works, the problem could be the plug.

2. If that didn't work, connect with your Surface, the power supply came with.

3. When the original power cord is plugged with your surface, charge it for 15 minutes. Then press on the power button to turn the Surface on.

Wake Up With Keyboard and Tablet Shortcuts

If it didn't wake up by recharging your surface, here are a few things to try.

Connect to a keyboard or use a keyboard that is integrated. Then press the+ Ctrl + Shift + B on Windows logo button.

If you are in tablet mode, the volume-up should be pressed three times as well as the volume-down buttons.

Force shutdown

- When you find it difficult to charge your device and other accessories like keyboard and tablet shortcuts.
- When your device refuses to switch on

In a situation where all the options above are not resolving the problem, make a complaint request to Microsoft.

How to Unfreeze Your Surface Pro

If you experience freezing in your Surface Pro, then these are the steps you should take:

1. Long Press the power button for about 10 seconds. This will turn off the device.

2. Switch your device back on by pressing the power button. The Surface logo should appear on the screen and your device

In any case where these steps are ineffective, you can then proceed to use the two button process for complete shutdown.

1. Long press the power button for about 30 seconds until your device switches off, then release the button.

2. Long press the increase volume button and the power button together for about 15 seconds. The screen may flash the Surface logo.

3. After you release the buttons, wait 10 seconds.

4. Press and release the power button to turn your Surface back on. You should see the Surface logo.

To unfreeze your Surface Pro 7 devices use the following steps;

1. To turn off your device, long press the power button for about 10 seconds and release.
2. To turn your Surface back on, press the power button. The Microsoft should appear on the screen.

In case the steps above don't work, long press the power button for about 20 seconds for your Surface to restart then release. You will see the Windows logo appear on the screen.

To boost the speed of a slow Surface use the following steps;

Use the following steps to check and troubleshoot your Surface when it is running slower than normal;

Power Mode Settings

Power mode enables you adjust the performance rate of your device for an optimized battery life. To access this setting, click on the battery icon displayed on the taskbar. switch the button on the slider to either **improve performance.**

To Cool Down an Overheating Surface

Change the position of your Surface to a more ventilated position. Observe for five minutes to see if there's any improvement in performance. Then connect your Surface charger.

If overheating occurs when running high performing apps at the same time, close some of the apps for some time for your Surface to cool down.

To restart your Surface

Click on Start > then click on Power > choose Restart.

To troubleshoot hardware issues

Identify hardware issues on your Surface, by running the following diagnostic tools that are available on your Windows operating system;

Windows Memory Diagnostic Tool

Check your Surface memory for optimum performance by running the Windows Memory Diagnostics

1. Type **memory** in the search box found in the taskbar. Then select **Windows Memory Diagnostic** from the list of options.

2. Click on **Restart now and check for problems (recommended).**

While your Surface is booting, the diagnostic tool runs and displays the results on the screen. After this your device will restart once the analysis has been completed.

Error Checking Tool

Error Checking tool enables you to check for malfunctions in your hard drive. To run this tool, use the following steps;

1. Launch **File Explorer** from the taskbar and choose **This PC**.

2. Long press the Windows key on your keyboard or right click on the Windows icon in the task bar. Then select **Properties**.

3. The next step will be to click on the **Tools** tab, and beneath **Error checking**, click on **Check**.

Simply follow the instructions displayed on your screen.

Unable to launch Windows on Surface

When you switch on your Surface and Windows fails to launch properly, you can follow these steps to rectify the issue. If Windows doesn't start correctly when you turn on your Surface, here are solutions for some of the more common screens that might appear.

- To Begin

- Screen Display
- Windows still won't come up

To Begin

Ensure your Surface is properly connected to a power supply. Also ensure to unplug all forms of accessories such as; microSD card, external monitor, adapters, e.t.c, from your device. If applicable, remove your Surface from the docking station.

Screen Display

When you turn on your Surface and Windows fails to launch properly, the following will display on your screen. To troubleshoot your Surface, choose the appropriate option from the list below and follow the instructions.

Black, blue, other-dark-colored, or backlit screen

Choose an option screen

Microsoft or Surface logo screen

Large thermometer icon

Automatic Repair screen

Large battery icon

Firmware interface (UEFI) configuration screen

Red screen or Red bar with Microsoft or Surface logo

American Megatrends TPM security options screen

Large padlock icon

Blank Screen Display

These are some of the common scenarios you will notice in this case;

- You may notice a blank black or blue screen without the Surface logo.

- **Getting devices ready** may be displayed on the screen or you will notice a spinning circle.

- Your Surface isn't responding when switched on.

For Blank black screen, follow these steps accordingly:

Solution 1: Update Installation

Large updates take about 20 minutes to complete installation, during which the screen may be black and blank. Give some time for installation to be completed.

Move to Solution 2 if the issue persists.

Solution 2: Force a shut down and restart

Solution 3: External Drive Recovery

To launch Windows from an external drive, connect your USB recovery drive to your Surface. After that long press the volume-down button simultaneously with the power button.

Let go of the buttons when the Surface logo displays on the screen.

Microsoft Or Surface Logo Screen

These are some of the common scenarios you will notice in this case;

- You may notice the Surface or Microsoft logo displayed on a black or blue screen with Windows refusing to launch.

- **Getting devices ready** may be displayed on the screen or you will notice a spinning circle.

Follow these steps accordingly to solve these issues:

Solution 1: Update Installation

Large updates take about 20 minutes to complete installation, during which the screen may be black and blank. Give some time for installation to be completed. Move to Solution 2 if the issue persists.

Solution 2: Force a shut down and restart

To find out how to force your Surface to shut down and restart, **see Force a shut down and restart your Surface**.

If this solves the issue ensure to update your Surface and Windows OS to the latest version. If issue persists, move to Solution 3.

Solution 3: External Drive Recovery

To launch Windows from an external drive, connect your USB recovery drive to your Surface. After that long press the volume-down button simultaneously with the power button.

Let go of the buttons when the Surface logo displays on the screen.

Automatic Repair Screen

These are some of the common scenarios you will notice in this case

- **Preparing Automatic Repair** and **Diagnosing your PC** will be displayed on a black background on your screen.
- You may also notice **Automatic Repair** or **Recovery** displayed on the screen.

Get Things DoneoFaster With Surface Pro

Translate Text on the Fly

In Word, highlight a few text, right-click it, and then select Translate. Select your preferred language to view the translation. Select Insert to include it in your document.

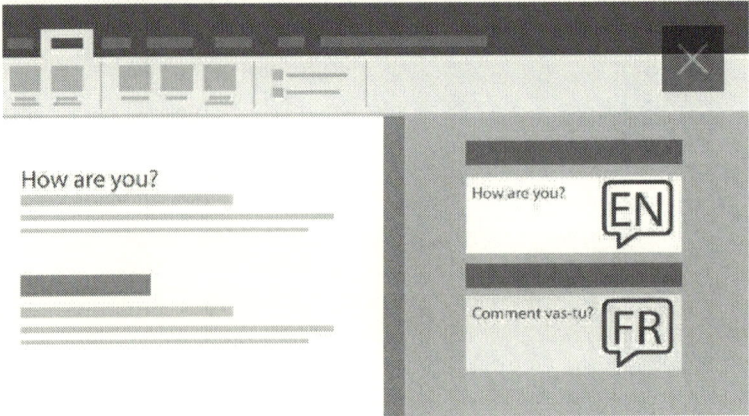

Fill Forms with a Click

Allow Microsoft Edge to complete your forms on the web.

To edit or increase your info, click on Settings and more, then select Settings, click on Passwords & autofill, select Manage forms.

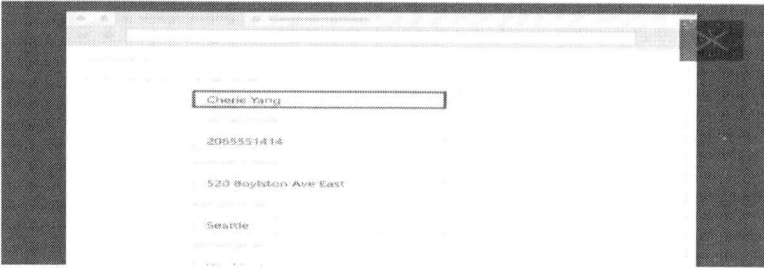

Fill Cells in a Flash

After typing in some entries; automatically, the remaining cells are completed by Excel. To confirm the suggestion, click on Enter.

First and last name	First name	Last Name
Nancy Smith	Nancy	Smith
Andy North	Andy	North
Jan Kotas	Jan	Kotas

Give Feedback with Surface Pen

Surface Pen allows you to mark up and edit PowerPoint, Excel, and Word files. Search for the Draw menu.

It makes giving feedback as prompt (and even enjoyable) as possible.

Jump Between Apps

To make a quick maneuver between apps. Put three fingers on your touchpad and make a right or left swipe to alternate between your open apps.

Save Time While You Type

To view text suggestions while you are typing, lick on Start, then Settings, then Devices, then Typing, then select Hardware keyboard, then select Show text suggestions as I type.

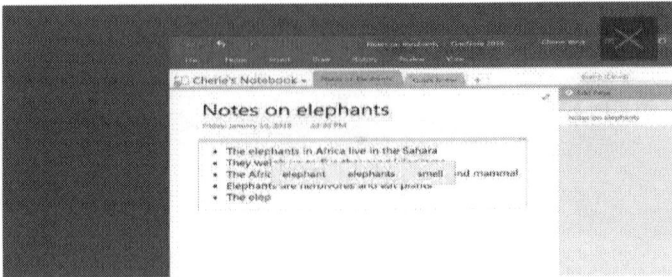

Lock your PC in a second

Ensure the safety of your PC. Click on Windows logo key and L simultaneously before you leave it.

Take Surface Pro 7 to Class

Take notes in OneNote

Make a tab for every class; then set pages for each task or date. Write down your thoughts and notes using your Surface Pen.

Make Notes on a Web Page

On Microsoft Edge, click on Settings and more, then select more tools, then Add Notes.

Write and draw anything you want on the page, and Share it with people across various platforms such as social media and email.

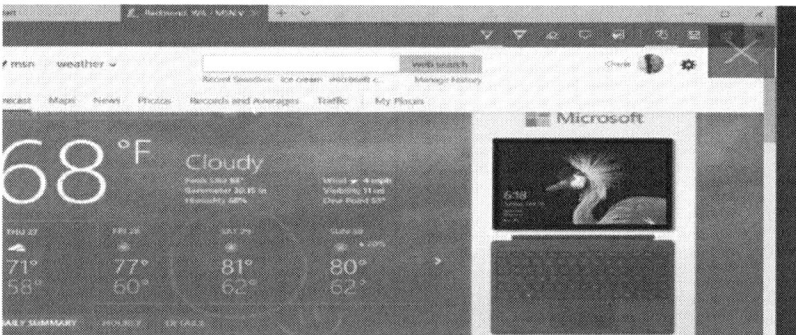

Write In Full Screen Mode

Remove every distraction. Open OneNote and click on Enter Full Screen Mode; draw or write using your Surface Pen, in the same way that you would if it were a book.

Leave Your Notebook At Home

Using your digital pen to write in OneNote is now almost the same as using a normal notebook. You would never lose it as it is saved automatically to OneDrive.

To insert grids or lines, open OneNote and click on View, then Rule Lines.

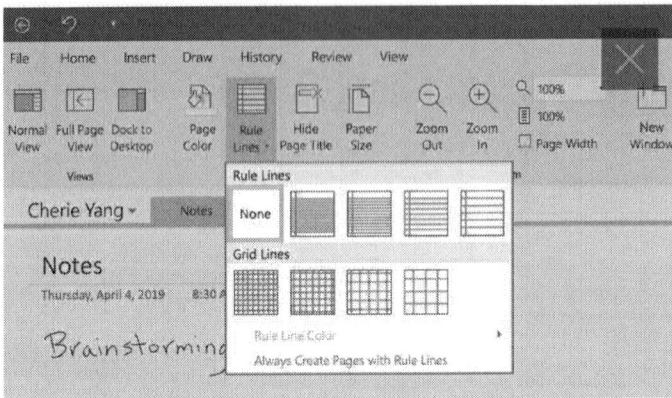

Record it

To save a lecture, click Insert, then Audio. After you are through, click on Stop. Every note that you write when the recording is going on will be saved to OneNote, and you can listen again next time while you review.

Replay notes

If you are finding it difficult to recall your line of thought, click on View, then Replay to help refresh your memory.

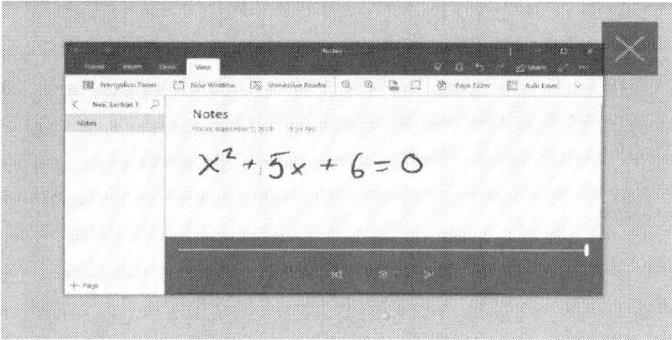

Turn Handwriting into Text

If you want to transfer notes from OneNote, click on Draw, then Lasso Select and make drawings around the handwriting. Then click on Ink to text. You can now copy and paste.

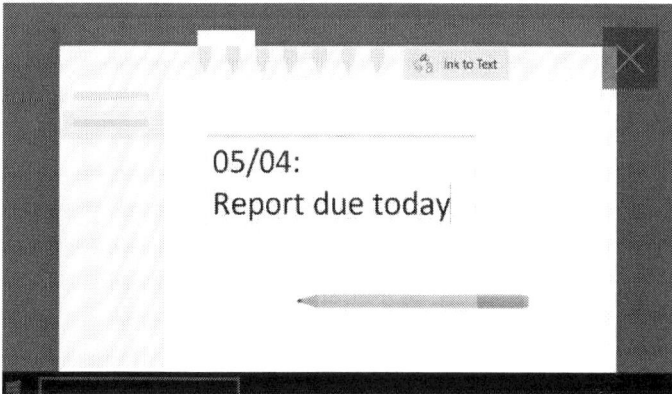

Let Onenote Do the Math

Jot down an equation using Surface Pen, then click on Draw, then Lasso Select and draw a circle around it. Click on Math, then Choose an action, and the solution is provided by OneNote!

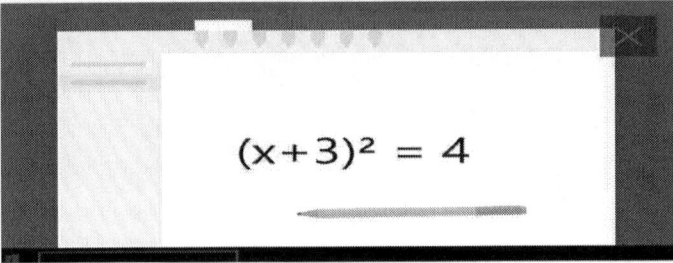

Use Onedrive to Collaborate

Simultaneously press E and Windows logo key to open File, and then click on OneDrive.

Drag a file, right-click on it, and then click on More OneDrive sharing options so that everyone can include their contributions.

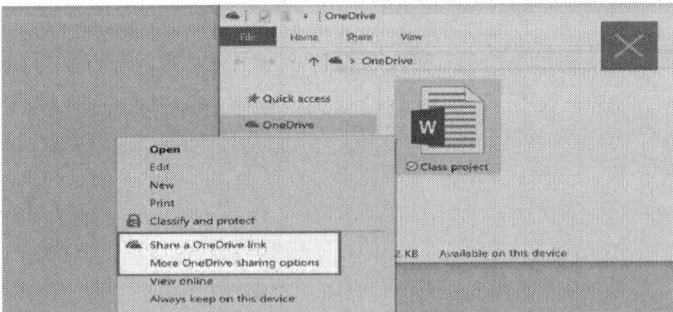

Work things out in a Skype call

Finding it hard to get the group together physically? Put a call through Skype. It is free using Wi-Fi.

Use Microsoft Teams to keep it all organized

Leave email and start using Microsoft Teams. Access your files on OneDrive, hold online conferences using Skype, or chat with the entire group or directly to whom you want. It includes all the things required for your group project.

Use Your Surface Pen

It doesn't matter if you are sketching a landscape, writing down important notes, or signing documents, the newly improved Surface Pen brings maximizes the potential of that activity.

Erase with Surface Pen

Turn over your Surface Pen and erase using the top button, similar to a pencil! Do this in Windows Ink Workspace.

Select things with Surface Pen

To select an item, move the Surface Pen on the screen while pressing the barrel button.

Scroll with your Surface Pen

It is hardly necessary to search for scroll bars again. Just as if you were using your finger, simply move Surface Pen upwards or downwards on the screen to scroll through a webpage.

Are you right-handed or left-handed?

Setting which hand you would write with helps Surface Pen to recognize your handwriting better.

Click on Start, then Settings, then Devices, then select Pen & Windows Ink.

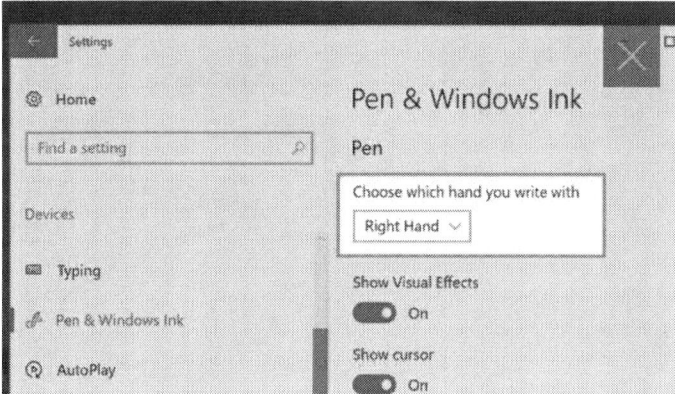

Make the Top Button Open the App You Want

Click on Start, then Settings, and then click on Devices, then Pen & Windows Ink. In the Pen shortcuts, select the app you wish to open.

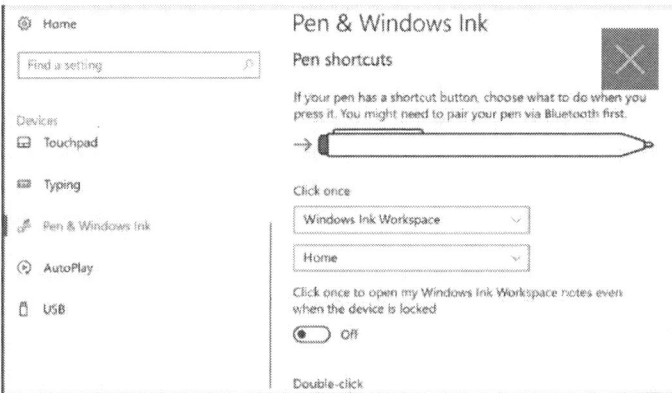

Find Your Missing Surface Pen

Click on Start, then Settings, then select Update & Security, click on Find my device to view the last time your pen was used and locate where it was at the time.

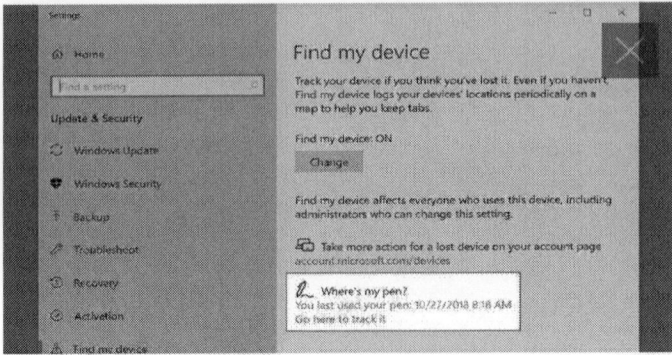

Color stress away with Surface Pen

From various researches, it has been shown that coloring can make you more focused and relieve anxiety.

Many coloring book apps that can be used with your Surface Pen can be downloaded in the Microsoft Store.

Writing as Meditative Practice

A few minutes of daily writing, in a notebook or in OneNote, can alleviate your worries and help you discover your real self. Write down anything you are thinking about. Do not stop when you are blank, simply write "I don't know what to write now" and find out where that leads.

Surface Pen

The surface pen enables you to write and draw naturally. It can also be used in interacting with your Surface touch screen just like when using a mouse. When your surface pen is not in use, you can stick it to the left side of your screen with the magnet.

1 Top button

2Right-click button

3. LED light

Tip: Before you can start using your surface pen especially when it's the first time, you must pair the pen with your surface device by taking the following steps:

i. Select the Start button on your PC.

ii. Select "Settings."

iii. Select "Devices."

iv. Select "Bluetooth & other devices."

v. Turn on "Bluetooth."

vi. Tap on "Add Bluetooth or other devices."

vii. Select "Bluetooth."

viii. Go to the top button of the pen, then press and hold it for five to seven seconds and release afterward. Once you release, the light available on the flat side of the pen will indicate a green light.

ix. A list of devices will be displayed, go ahead and select the "Surface Pen" from the list.

x. Follow the on-screen instructions that come up.

xi. Select "Done."

Customize the Sensitivity of Your Surface Pen

Launch the Surface app and click on Pen. Correct the quantity of Windows Ink deposited once you modify the pressure of your Pen on the screen.

The Surface Pro Camera and App

Launch the Camera app on your Surface and take a photo. Select the picture from the Camera Roll and click Share to transfer it to and app or send it to people.

Add Notes on a Photo with Your Surface

Insert your thoughts in a photo. Launch the Camera app and take a picture. Make a selection from the Camera roll, then click on Edit & Create, then click on Draw. Use your Surface Pen to include notes then click on save a copy.

Draw On a Selfie or Any Photo

Click on Photos, choose your preferred picture, then click on Edit & Create, then click on Draw. Select a drawing tool, then draw your mouse, finger, or even a paired pen.

Using Paint 3D, draw any object using 3D tools or pick your preference from Remix 3D. Click on Art tools , and pick a brush and color. Rotate Surface Dial while you are filling the object with colors.

Check the Power of Your Surface Accessory

Assess the battery level of your Surface Pen or Mouse in the Surface app. To view further info, click on Battery level.

Find Your Serial Number

Open the Surface app, click on Your Surface. You can view your serial number, and other additional details about your Surface there, so it is simple to copy and paste when needed.

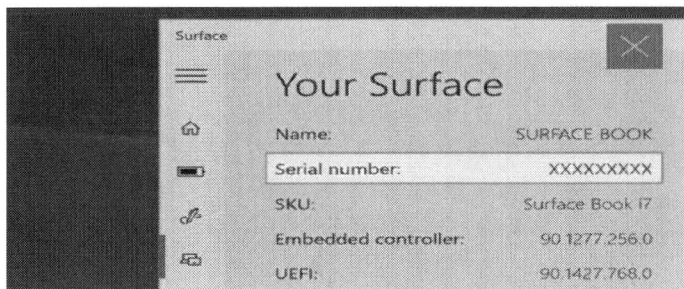

Settings of Screen Resolutions on Microsoft Surface

There are millions of pixels packed in Microsoft Surface devices hence for their high efficiency in delivering quality display that can be compare to that of the human eye. But there are some issues that arise when working with some software especially some old apps that have no app scaling awareness.

So for developers to amend this problem, they need to redesign their software to fit with high DPI. You can as well adjust the resolution of your display into a 100% display scaling in other to tackle this problem. However, there is no 3:2 resolution option available in Windows 10 except the default maximum resolution as you can see in the picture below.

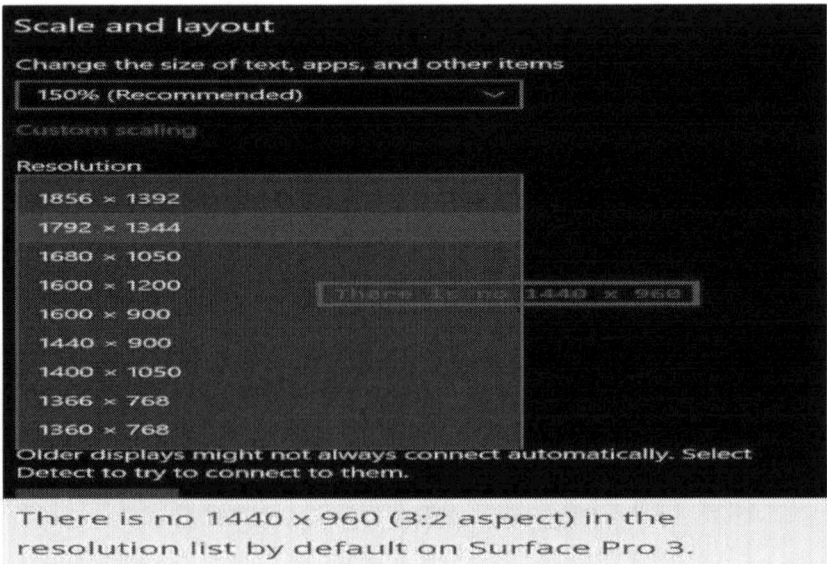

Scale and layout

Change the size of text, apps, and other items

150% (Recommended)

Custom scaling

Resolution

1856 × 1392
1792 × 1344
1680 × 1050
1600 × 1200
1600 × 900
1440 × 900
1400 × 1050
1366 × 768
1360 × 768

There is no 1440 × 960

Older displays might not always connect automatically. Select Detect to try to connect to them.

There is no 1440 x 960 (3:2 aspect) in the resolution list by default on Surface Pro 3.

- The reason for custom resolutions on Microsoft Surface?
- Resolution for Microsoft Surface screen
- Learn how to include custom resolutions to the system resolution list
- How to apply your new custom resolution
- Other ways you can take

The Reason for Custom Resolutions on Microsoft Surface

In some situations, you may need a custom resolution. Here is a few of those:

1 Some apps do no support DPI and a custom resolution will be required.

2 You might want to work on some problems that occur when working on two or more displays.

3 If you want to optimize the performance of the game with a smaller resolution and a right 3:2 aspect ratio.

Resolution for Microsoft Surface Screen

When you want to add a custom resolution, here is some native resolution scaling that stand at 100% for you.

Device Name	Native Resolution & Scaling	Resolution at 100% Scaling
Surface Go	1800 x 1200 (150%)	1200 x 800 (100%)
Surface Pro 3	2160 x 1440 (150%)	1440 x 960 (100%)
Surface Pro 4 / Pro 5 / Pro 6	2736 x 1824 (200%)	1368 x 912 (100%)
Surface Laptop / Laptop 2	2256 x 1504 (150%)	1504 x 1002 (100%)
Surface Book / Book 2 13"	3000 x 2000 (200%)	1500 x 1000 (100%)
Surface Book 2 15"	3240 x 2160 (200%)	1620 x 1080 (100%)
Surface Studio	4500 x 3000 (200%)	2250 x 1500 (100%)

Learn how to include custom resolutions to the system resolution list

A tool very good at managing custom resolution, ladies and gentlemen: CRU. To get this:

1 Download the CRU (Custom Resolution Utility).

2 Extract the downloaded file.

3 Custom Resolution Utility files

Launch the CRU tool.

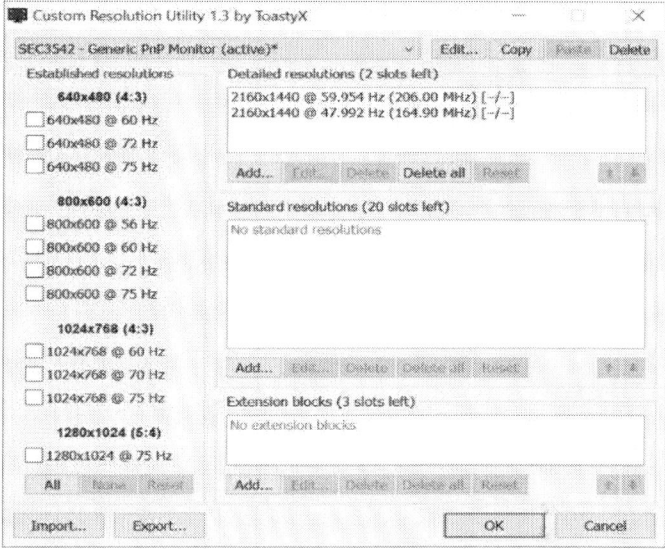

4 Press the Add button under detailed resolutions to add a custom resolution

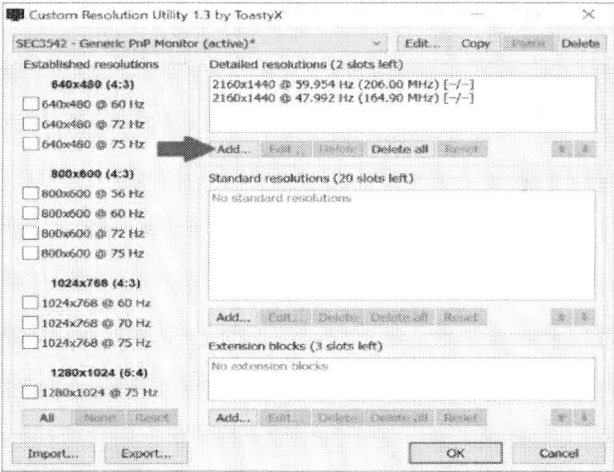

5 Set the values of your horizontal and vertical resolution of your choice. My own settings on my Surface Pro is 1440 for horizontal and 960 for vertical.

Detailed Resolution ✕

Timing: Manual ⌄ | Copy | Paste | Reset

Parameters

	Horizontal		Vertical	
Active:	1440	pixels	960	
Front porch:	48	pixels	3	lines
Sync width:	32	pixels	10	lines
⦿ Back porch:	80	pixels	28	lines
◯ Blanking:	160	pixels	41	lines
◯ Total:	1600	pixels	1001	lines
Sync polarity:	+ ⌄		− ⌄	

Frequency

⦿ Refresh rate:	59.954	Hz	Actual: 59.958 Hz
◯ Horizontal:	60.018	kHz	Actual: 60.018 kHz
◯ Pixel clock:	96.03	MHz	☐ Interlaced

OK | Cancel

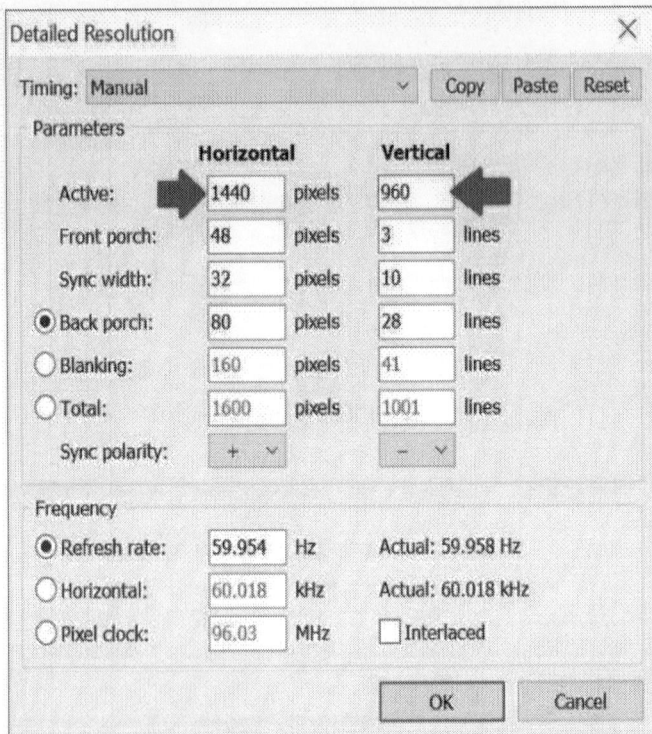

6 PRESS OK to close the Detailed Resolution dialog.

7 Press OK again and save changes.

8 Restart your computer to affect the updated settings.

Set your added custom resolution when you are done restarting your Surface.

1 Launch Settings > System > Display.

2 Select your new custom resolution (1440 x 960) under New Resolution.

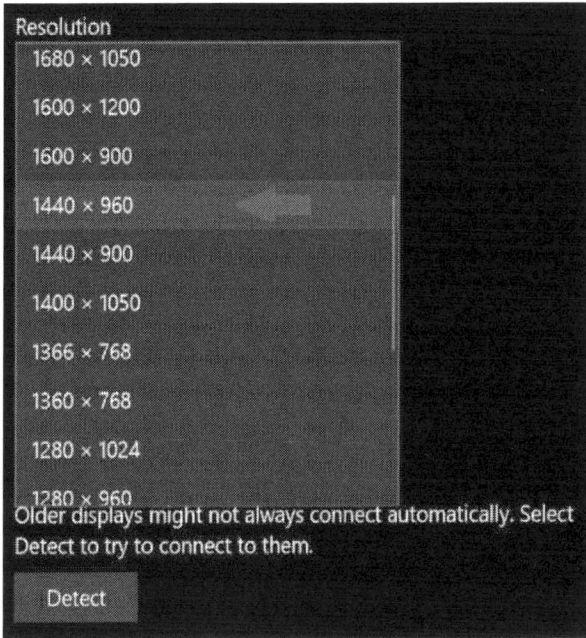

Resolution
1680 × 1050
1600 × 1200
1600 × 900
1440 × 960
1440 × 900
1400 × 1050
1366 × 768
1360 × 768
1280 × 1024
1280 × 960

Older displays might not always connect automatically. Select Detect to try to connect to them.

Detect

3 Press Keep Changes to accept your new resolution.

Configuration of Surface Mobile Mouse with Microsoft Mouse and Keyboard Center

You do not want to miss the tips for customizing your mouse settings for better usage. To configure the Surface Mobile Mouse's DPI value settings, right and left click, scrolling behavior and wheel button click.

Microsoft Surface Mobile Mouse is superb for its stylish appearance; it is cost effective, ultra-thin and set to fit to both hands.

It consists of all the three quality tone-on-tone colors and also the platinum, Cobalt blue and Burgundy. The scroll has been made to suit the new optimized metallic wheel for better accuracy and comfort-ability.

One of the important components of the Microsoft Surface Mobile Mouse is its efficiency to configure the majority of its commands. Which are button remapping that gives both the right and left handed users an equal experience.

But to make a configuration for this option, it requires that you install the Microsoft Surface Mobile Mouse and the Keyboard Center on your Computer.

In this write-up, we will teach you how you can remap and configure the right and left click, the scrolling performance, wheel button press and the DPI settings.

1 Configuring Surface Mobile Mouse with Microsoft Mouse and Keyboard Center

If you want to configure Surface Mobile Mouse, ensure that the following has been done.

- You must have downloaded the Microsoft Mouse and Keyboard Center on your PC and installed them. Find on how to download and install the Microsoft Mouse and Keyboard Center here.

- You must have successfully connected the Surface Mobile Mouse to your PC. Find here on how to connect a Surface Mobile Mouse to your PC here.

- You can now continue to launch the Microsoft Mouse and Keyboard Center on the start menu. If you are doing it rightly, Surface Mobile Mouse configurations interface will appear as below:

You are now ready to begin.

2 Remapping left button on Surface Mobile Mouse

Swapping between the right and left click is one of the fundamental features. This can be done with Surface Mobile Mouse. Press the Action key on Surface Mobile Mouse to remap the left button.

1 Choose Left button on the main configuration page.

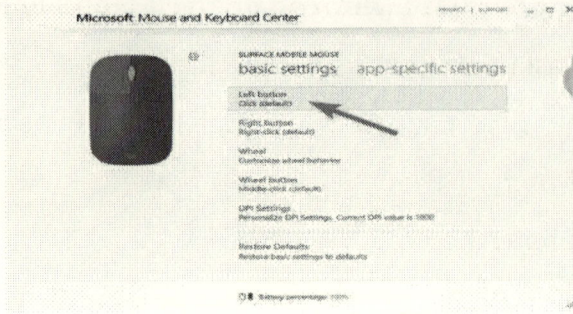

2 You will be taken to the Left button configuration page with the below options.

You can remap the '**Left button**' with the below settings at the "Left button" settings page:

- Tap (default) – Maintain the default click action.
- Right-click – reset it to a right-click action for the left-handed people.

3 Remapping the right button on Surface Mobile Mouse

For similar reasons on Surface Mobile Mouse, there may be need to change from right click to left click. This is how to remap your right click button:

1 Chose Right button on the main configuration page.

2 You will be taken to the Right button configuration page with the below options.

You can remap the 'Right button' with the below settings at the "Right" button settings page:

- Tap (default) – Maintain the default click action.

- Right Click– reset it to a left-click action for the left-handed people.

4 Configuration of the scroll performance on Surface Mobile Mouse

You can also customize the scrolling behavior of Surface Mobile Mouse as well in the Microsoft Mouse and Keyboard Center.

To do so:

The scrolling performance can be altered on Surface Mobile Mouse and on Microsoft and Keyboard Center. To carry this out:

1 Choose Wheel on the configuration page.

2 You will be taken to the Wheel settings configuration page with the below options.

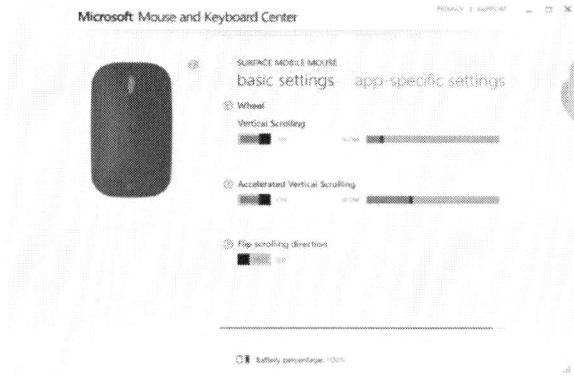

You can turn on or off and customize a specific value for the below scrolling performance on the configuration page:

- Vertical Scrolling – ON/OFF the vertical scrolling (2 fingers swipe up or down). Also, a scrolling speed can be set.

- Accelerated Vertical Scrolling – This lets you a longer distance in a document when scrolling quickly. This is very much needed when scrolling along a large document or web pages.

- Flip Scrolling Direction – It reverse the vertical scrolling direction.

Configuring the "Wheel button click" on Surface Mobile Mouse

A specific action can be assigned for the wheel button in Microsoft Mouse and Keyboard Center. Here is how you can go about it:

1,Choose Wheel button on the configuration page.

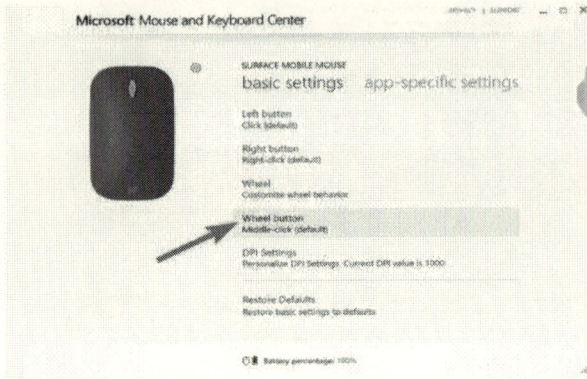

You will be taken to the Wheel settings configuration page with the below options.

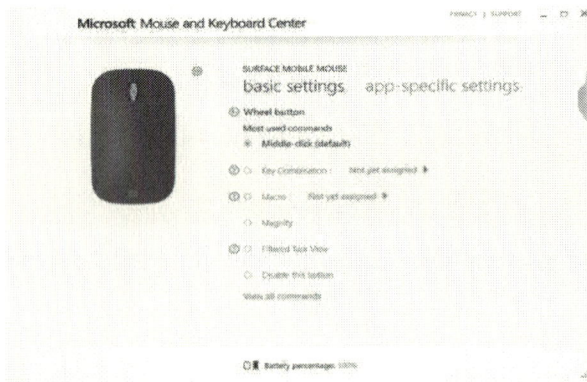

The actions you can assign for the "wheel button click" on Surface Mobile Mouse are 6 different types:

1. 1st Option: Middle-click (default) – Make use of the default middle-click action (known as scroll wheel click).

2. 2nd Option: Key Combination – It lets you specify a key combination interface manually, see below:

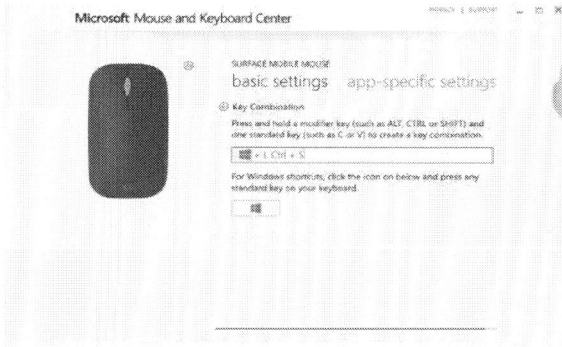

Microsoft Mouse and Keyboard Center

3. 3rd Option 3: Macro: This is a product of events (like mouse clicks, keystrokes, and time delays) that you can utilize to support the repetitive tasks and sequences which can be difficult or long to execute manually. When you are done creating a Macro, it can be assigned to a button or mouse for easy run.

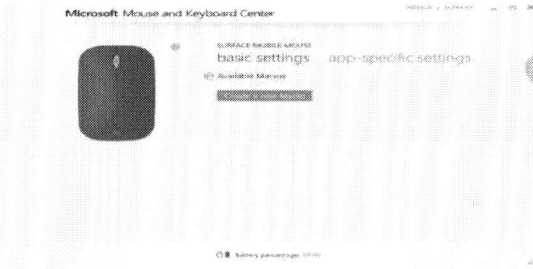

4. 4th Option: See all commands: it lets you map the wheel button click into one of the below commands:

131

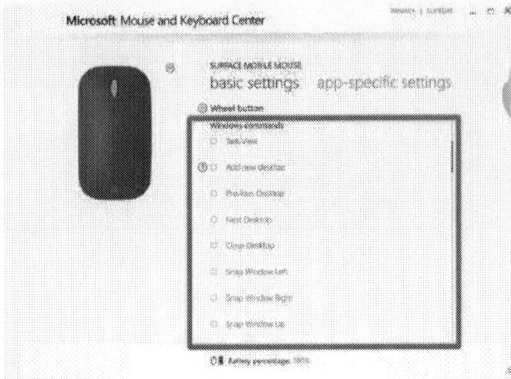

5. 5th Option: Deactivate this button.

A preset commands that are available for assigning are as the following.

1 **Windows commands**

- Task View
- Add new desktop
- Previous Desktop
- Next Desktop
- Close Desktop
- Snap Windows Left
- Snap Windows Right
- Snap Windows Up
- Snap Windows Down
- Open Action Center
- Open Cortana
- Show/Hide App Commands
- Search
- Connect

- Settings
- Go to Windows Start
- Close
- Exit Program
- Show/Hide Desktop
- Next Window
- Previous Window

2 Browser Commands

- Browser Back
- Browser Forward

3 Content Commands

- Copy (Ctrl+C)
- Cut (Ctrl+X)
- Delete
- Paste (Ctrl+V)
- Undo (Ctrl+Z)
- Redo (Ctrl+Y)
- Page Up
- Page Down
- Print Screen

4 Document commands

- New
- Open

5 Key commands

- Alt
- Ctrl
- Shift
- Enter

6 Configuring the DPI settings on Surface Mobile Mouse

A specific DPIs can be specified as (dots per linear inch) value for Surface Mobile Mouse for adaption to you environment and preference. Here is how to do it:

1. Choose DPI settings on the main configuration page.

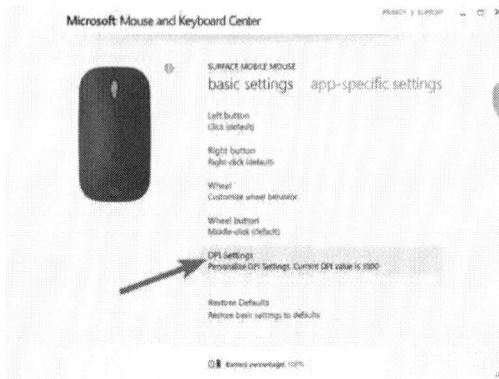

2 You will be taken to the DPI settings configuration page with
the   below   options.

A value in between 400 to 1800 can be indicated in the
configuration page. This will take an immediate effect for you to
know that will work perfectly.

7 Restoring the default settings on Surface Mobile Mouse

In case you have made a wrong configuration and now you want
to get it back to default, there is a way to do that.

Follow the instruction below:

1. After the changes from default have been made, the
   configuration will display a new option known as Restore
   Default which will let you reset all customized settings back to
   default. Click on this option to get it done.

2 It will display yet again another 2 buttons, press Restore to restore all the default settings.

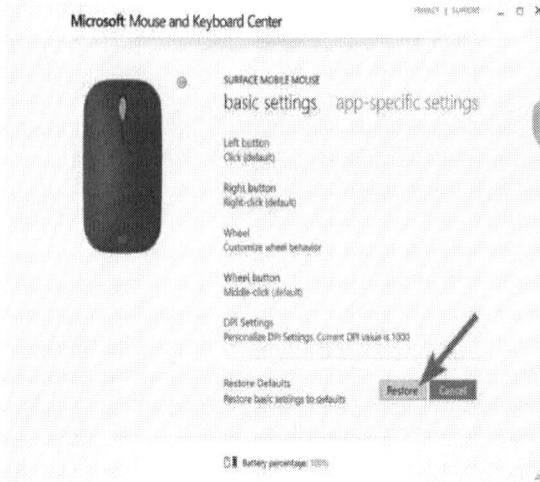

Chapter 19: How to connect a Surface Mobile Mouse to your computer

Are you having a problem on how to connect your Surface Mobile Mouse to your Surface or computer? Below instructions will guide you through in detail.

The Surface Mobile Mouse is one of the latest cost effective mice innovated by Microsoft. It came to life together with the Microsoft Surface Pro 7 on the 10th of July, 2018. It is handy, light and comes in three quality tone-on-tone colors: platinum, Cobalt blue and Burgundy.

It fits for all kinds of mobile computing such as the Microsoft Surface Pro 7, Laptop, Pro Book and other laptops.

This mouse comes with the Bluetooth low energy version 4.0 or 4.1 which means you can have it connected to either desktops or laptops. Just ensure that there is a Bluetooth adapter or Bluetooth module that comes with your computer.

Continue reading to learn how to make a connection from your Surface Mobile Mouse to your computer.

Note: Surface RT and all other Surface devices come with a Bluetooth module which supports the Bluetooth low energy version 4.0. This allows you to connect Surface Mobile Mouse to any other Surface devices.

How to connect Surface Mobile Mouse via Swift Pair Feature

Bluetooth Swift Pair is of the new features you will find on Windows 10 and other latest Bluetooth devices. This function gives the user fast and easy connecting supported close on Bluetooth devices through a basic notification. Surface Mobile Mouse is also in support of this feature which means that you have to know how to make use of this feature perfectly. Follow the instruction below:

1st Step: **Entering Pairing Mode**

- First to do is to check if your computer supports Bluetooth LE 4.0 and Windows 10.
- Be certain to turn it on by tapping the Bluetooth button below the mouse on Surface Mobile Mouse. The LED light will turn on accordingly.

- Long press on the Bluetooth button say for 3-5 seconds. The LED light below the mouse will start blinking until they are paired.

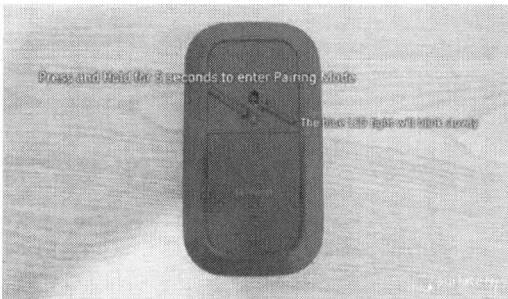

2nd Step: **How to accept the Connection Request on your Computer**

1 Ensure that the Surface Mobile Mouse is near your PC.

2 Windows will show you a notification in a few seconds..

3 Tap the Connect button to begin pairing.

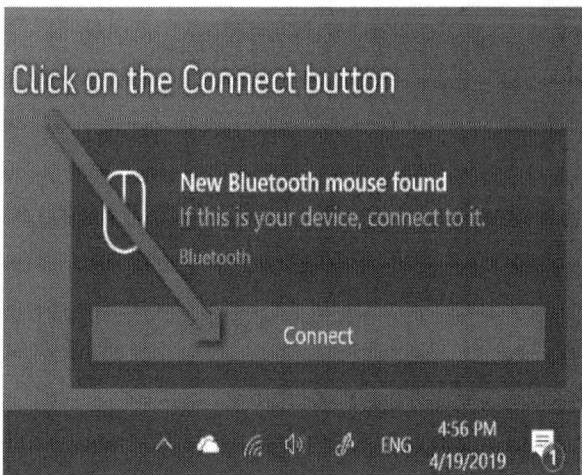

Click on the Connect button

New Bluetooth mouse found
If this is your device, connect to it.
Bluetooth

Connect

4 It will display a message to inform you after it has successfully connected your Surface Mobile Mouse.

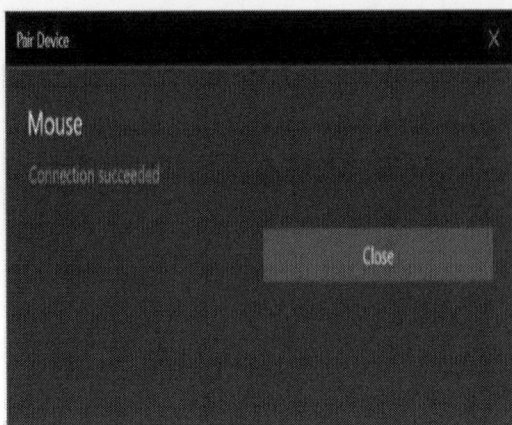

Pair Device   X

Mouse

Connection succeeded

Close

How to connect Surface Mobile Mouse via Bluetooth Setting

If the 1st option does not work properly, there is another, try connecting with the old method pairing available for you in Bluetooth settings. Follow the below instructions to guide you.

1. Place the Surface Mobile Mouse in Pairing Mode by following the above steps.

2. Click or press the Action Center icon, make a long hold on or right-click the Bluetooth button on your PC, Choose Go to Settings

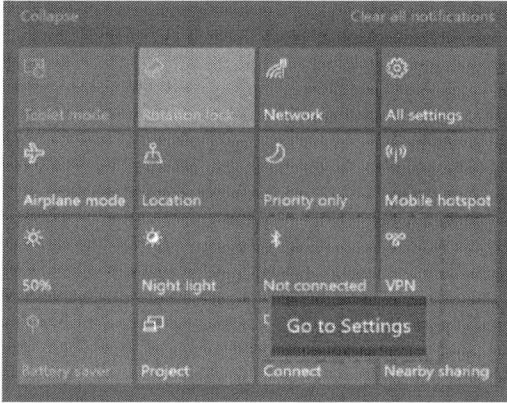

3 Tap "Add Bluetooth or other device"

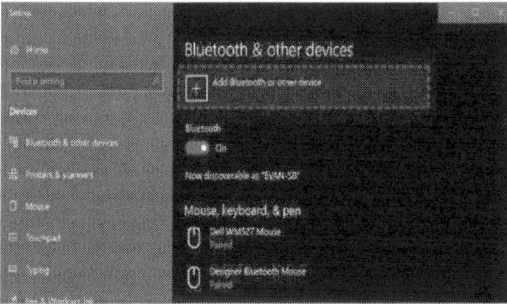

4 Choose Bluetooth

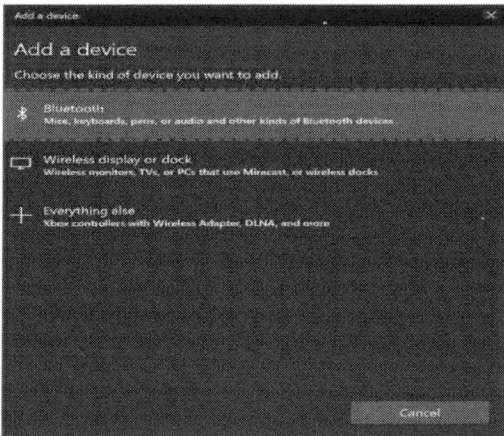

5 Choose "Surface Mobile Mouse"

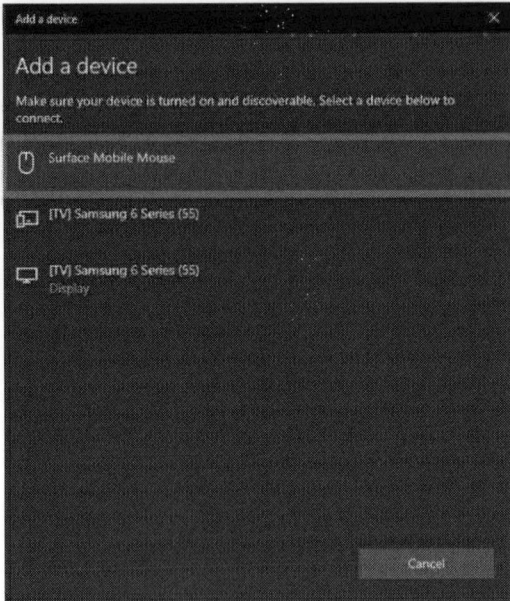

6 Tap Done

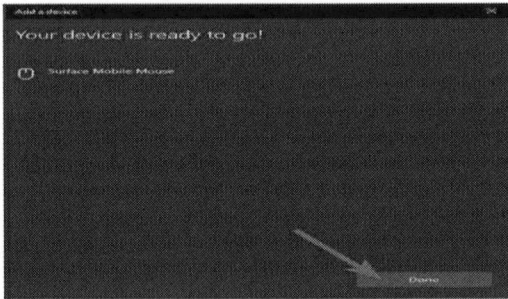

Surface Mobile Mouse is now ready to use on your Windows 10 PC.

Alternatively

Connecting Surface Precision Mouse via Bluetooth

Microsoft Surface Precision can be connected to a max of 3 computers and you can also configure to switch between computers automatically. This is how you can connect your Microsoft Surface Mouse to the computer wirelessly:

1 Your computer must support Bluetooth LE 4.0 or turn it on later.

2 Switch it on by using the power switch on the bottom of your Surface Precision Mouse.

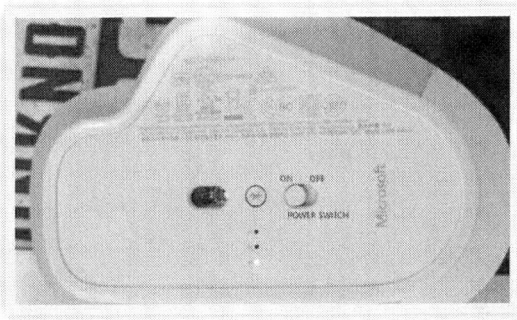

3 Tap the Bluetooth button to select the connection from the 3 connections you prefer to use.

4 Make a long hold on the Bluetooth key for 3-5 seconds. The selected connection slot light will start to blink until it gets paired.

5 Tap the Action Center icon, make a long hold or right click the Bluetooth key and choose Go to settings.

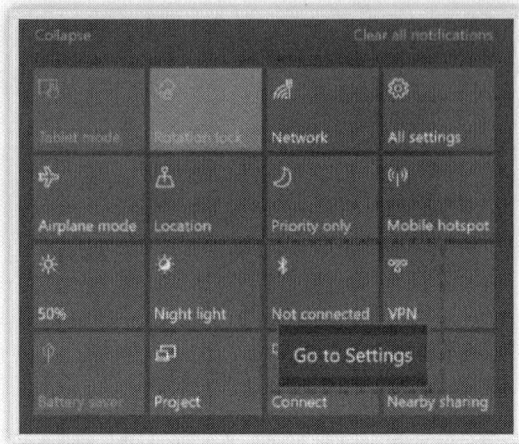

6 Press "**Add Bluetooth or other device**"

7 choose Bluetooth

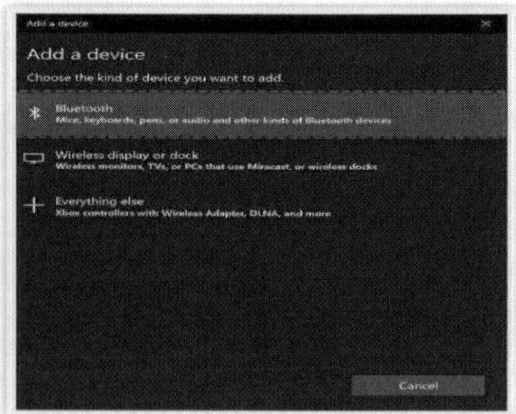

8 Choose "**BTLE Precision Mouse**"

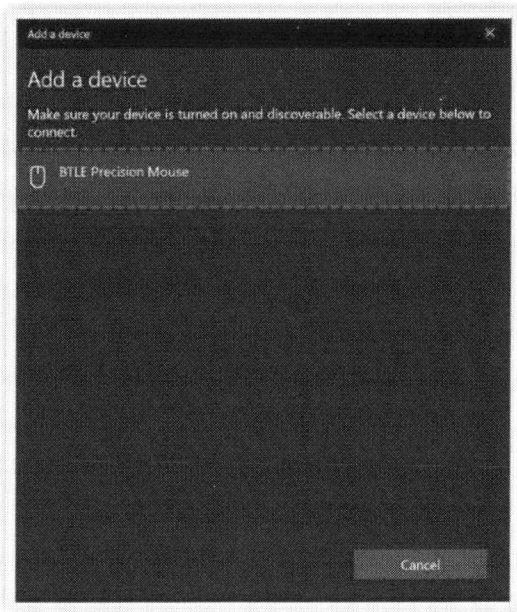

9 Tap Done

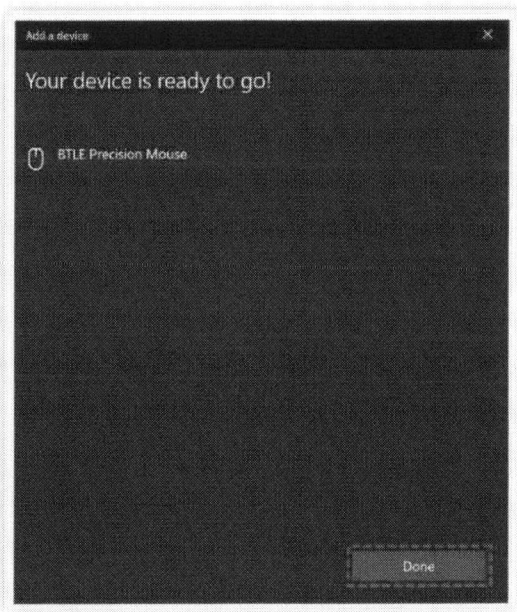

Surface Precision Mouse can now be used on your Windows 10 PC.

Update Surface firmware and Windows 10

Two sorts of updates keep your Surface playing out its best: Surface updates hardware, otherwise called firmware, and Windows 10 software updates. The two software install as they become accessible.

Before you start updating

Have your Surface Type Cover or Surface docking station attached, so it gets the most recent updates, as well.

Ensure you have a web connection, ideally Wi-Fi or Ethernet, which are the best for downloads. If you can't install updates, this may be due to a connection issue. Fix network connection problems in Windows.

If you can't use Wi-Fi, there are a few other options:

• You can use an Ethernet connection with the Surface Dock or Ethernet to USB connector.

• If you have a LTE-enabled device, turn off **Set as metered connection** with get all updates over your mobile broadband connection. Find support with metered web connection.

Plug your Surface into an outlet, and ensure your Surface is charged to a minimum of 40 percent before installing updates. Keep your Surface connected and turned on while it's updating.

Update Windows 10

After following the planning steps, see Check for Windows updates to see accessible updates and deal with your alternatives.

Update Surface Drivers And Firmware

After following the preparation steps, if you can't check Windows Update, download update files manually for any Surface device.

To choose and update your Surface device, see Download drivers and firmware for Surface.

Note

Installation time differs, and it is contingent upon the speed of the web, the quantity of updates, and the size of the update files.

Issues installing updates?

If updates won't install, and shows you an error message, or your Surface stops while it's updating, here are a couple of things to attempt.

• Run the Windows Update troubleshooter

• Check your date and time settings

• Charge your battery

• Restart your Surface

• Install Surface updates manually

Run the Windows Update Troubleshooter

In case you're experiencing difficulty installing an update, do the following:

Check Your Date And Time Settings

If your date and time settings aren't right, you may see Windows Update error **80072F8F** when checking for updates, or updates may not install effectively.

To check your date and time settings, go to **Start** , and select **Settings** > **Time** and **language**.

Charge Your Battery

Ensure your battery is charged to a minimum of 40 percent before attempting to install updates.

If you see Windows Update error 8024004C, or if your Surface battery won't charge over 40 percent, remove and reinstall the battery driver. Here's how:

1. Install your Surface.

2. Select the search box enclosed in the taskbar, enter **device manager**, and in the search results, select **Device Manager**.

3. Choose the arrow next to the **Batteries** category.

4. Double tap **Microsoft ACPI-Compliant Control Method Battery**, and under the **Driver** tab, select **Uninstall** > **OK**.

5. Go to **Start**, and choose **Power** > **Restart**.

Restarting will reinstall the driver for you.

If the battery charges over 40 percent after you reinstall the driver, take a step at installing updates once more.

Restart your Surface

Caution

Intruding on updates while they're in progress could harm your Surface. If an update is slowed down and your Surface doesn't restart consequently, wait for a minimum of 20 minutes before attempting to restart your Surface yourself.

In case you're seeing any of these errors, restarting your Surface may fix the issue:

• Update error 80248007

• Update installation freezes for over 20 minutes

• Update remains on "Getting Devices Ready..." screen for over 20 minutes.

• Update remains on "Please wait while we install a system update" screen for over 20 minutes

• Update history shows "pending restart"

• Update history shows update "failed"

If you get one of these errors, attempt each of the restart solution below, within the order listed.

Solution 1: Restart your Surface

Go to **Start**, and choose **Power** > **Restart (or Update and restart)**.

After your Surface restarts, install updates once more. In case you're having an issue, attempt Solution 2.

Solution 2: Force a shut down

Force a shut down and restart your Surface. After your Surface restarts, install updates once more. In case you're experiencing difficulty installing updates, your Surface may require service.

Install Surface Updates Manually

In case you're experiencing difficulties or any issues while installing Surface Updates, then download the update file and have it installed manually.

Notes

•   The update files are solely for hardware equipment and firmware. You can't install Windows updates along these lines.

•   You cannot download and install Surface updates manually on Surface Pro .

Download a Recovery Image For Your Surface

Your Surface comes with Windows recovery data that you can use to revive your Surface or reset it to its factory condition. Continuously attempt to do that first before downloading a recovery image.

What you need

To download the recovery image, you will need a USB drive. For Surface RT and Surface 2, your USB drive ought to be at least 8 GB in size. For all other Surface models, your USB drive ought to be a minimum of 16 GB.

All USB recovery drives must be formatted to FAT32 before loading a recovery image.

Create a USB recovery drive

① Select your Surface device

Sign in to choose your device

| Sign in |

or

Choose a product and enter its serial number

Product

| Select a Surface product ⌄ |

Serial number *

| |

| Continue |

Creating and Utilizing A USB Recovery Drive For Surface

If your Surface won't begin, or if the recovery information has been removed, you can use your USB recovery drive to access recovery tools and tackle issues.

Ordinarily, your Surface comes with Windows recovery information that enables you to refresh it or reset it to its factory condition. In any case, if your machine won't begin, that is the point at which you need the solutions below.

Note

If your Surface starts, follow the steps below to Restore or reset Surface first.

Discover the situation that fits your issue and afterward select the answer for more information:

Download and make a factory recovery image for your Surface

A downloaded recovery drive image lets you reset your Surface to its factory settings and can assist you with troubleshooting and fixing issues with your Surface device.

If your Surface isn't working and you don't have another Windows 10 device that you can use to download the factory recovery image, you might have a USB recovery drive sent to you.

Important

Creating a recovery drive will erase everything that is kept on your USB drive. Ensure you're using a blank USB drive, or make sure to move any vital information on your USB drive to another different device before using it to make a recovery drive.

1. Ensure your Surface is turned off and connected, and afterward insert the USB recovery drive into the USB port. (Use a USB 3.0 drive if you can.)

2. Within the search box on the taskbar, type **recovery drive**, and afterward select **Create a recovery drive or Recovery Drive** from the list of results. You may be asked to enter an administrator password or affirm your decision.

3. In the User **Account Control** box, select **Yes**.

4. Make sure to clear the Backup **system files to the recovery drive** check box and afterward select **Next**.

5. Select your **USB drive**, and afterward select **Next** > **Create**. A few utilities should be duplicated to the recovery drive, so this may take a couple of minutes.

6. At the point when the recovery drive is prepared, select **Finish**.

7. Double tap the recovery image .zip file that you recently downloaded to open it.

8. Select all the files from the recovery image folder, copy them to the USB recovery drive you created, and afterward select **Choose to replace the files in the destination**

9. When the documents have completed the process of copying, select the Safely **Remove Hardware and Eject Media symbol** on the taskbar, and remove your USB.

The most effective method to reset your Surface to factory settings using a downloaded recovery image.

Important

A reset returns your Surface to its default settings. It erases all your own documents, resets your settings, and removes all applications that you installed

Note

Ensure you get access to the product keys and installing files for any desktop applications, for example, Microsoft Office, that you intend to reinstall after the reset.

1. Ensure your Surface is turned off and connected, and afterward insert the USB recovery drive into the USB port.

2. Press and hold the volume-down button while you press and unleash the power button.

3. At the point when the Microsoft or Surface logo shows up, press the volume-down button.

4. When prompted, select the language and keyboard format your need.

5. Select **Troubleshoot**, and afterward select **Recover from a drive**. When you're prompted for a recovery key, select **Skip** this drive at the base of the screen.

Note:

Ensure you choose the Troubleshoot option on this screen. Try not to choose the **Use a device** option. If you select the Use a device option, your Surface will reboot from the USB recovery drive again and the reset procedure will begin once again.

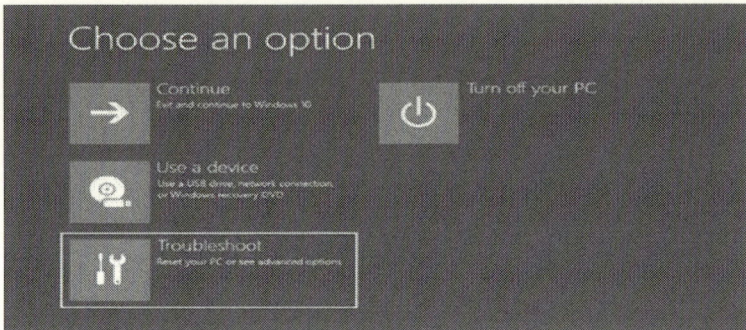

6. Make a choice between **Just remove my files or Fully clean the drive.**

The alternative to erase the drive is more secure however it takes much longer. For instance, in case you're reusing your Surface, you should clean the drive. In case you're keeping your Surface, you simply need to delete your files

7. Select **Recover**.

Surface restarts and shows the Surface logo while the reset procedure proceeds. This can take a few moments.

Creating and Utilizing Your Own USB Recovery Drive

Window comes with an inherent tool to create a USB recovery drive. To make one, you should use an external USB drive with enough usable space for all your recovery information.

Important

Creating a recovery drive will erase everything that is kept on your USB drive. Ensure to move any vital information on your USB drive to another different storage device before using it to make a recovery drive.

Once you've finished making the recovery drive, make sure to eject the drive using the **Safely Remove Hardware and Eject Media symbol** on the Windows taskbar.

Important

If you decide to erase your recovery segment, you'll need your USB recovery drive if you ever need to refresh or reset your Surface. Ensure to keep it in an exceeding safe place. It's best not to use the recovery drive to store different files or information.

Note

You can likewise use the Surface USB recovery drive if you see the Windows prompts for installation files when attempting to refresh or reset under **Start** > **Settings** > **Update and security** > **Recovery**.

If the USB recovery drive does not perform well on your Surface

If you can't boot from your USB recovery drive or don't see the **Recovery from a drive** option, you may need to make sure that the **boot-from-USB** function within the Surface BIOS is enabled. You can design the boot order so the USB drive is the primary choice.

Download drivers and firmware for Surface

Select your Surface model from the list below, then select the attached for the most recent firmware and drivers for sound, display, Ethernet, and Wi-Fi for your Surface.

You will be redirected to the details page of the Download Center for your device. Multiple downloads might be accessible, contingent upon the product you select.

• If you don't have the foggiest idea about your Surface model, select the search box on the taskbar and type **Surface**, select the **Surface** application from the menu, then select **Your Surface**. Your model will be listed on the screen that shows up.

• To find out the version and build the Windows you're utilizing, select **Start** > **Settings** > **System** > **About**, then look below **Windows Specifications** to locate your operating version and OS build number.

- To update your Surface with the most recent drivers and firmware from the Download Center, select **the .msi file** name that matches your Surface model and version of Windows.

If there's not a .msi that compares to the build of Windows 10 you have installed, select the .msi document that is nearest to (yet at the same time lower than) your build number.

For Surface Pro 7, go to https://www.microsoft.com/en-us/download/details.aspx?id=100419

Imaging Support

In case you're an IT specialist and you are planning or updating custom Windows images for your Surface devices, download imaging files from the Download Center to make sure that your image utilizes the most recent firmware and drivers.

If you're building a replacement reference image to be deployed, transfer the .msi package, which might be foreign into System Center Configuration Manager, Microsoft readying Toolkit, or alternative readying tools.

Note from the Author

Hope you find this guide useful. If you do, please leave a review on Amazon. Thanks in Advance.

Made in the USA
Coppell, TX
01 July 2020